Oliver Cromwell

VIP

Very Interesting People

Bite-sized biographies of Britain's most fascinating historical figures

1.	**William Shakespeare**	*Peter Holland*
2.	**George Eliot**	*Rosemary Ashton*
3.	**Charles Dickens**	*Michael Slater*
4.	**Charles Darwin**	*Adrian Desmond, James Moore, and Janet Browne*
5.	**Isaac Newton**	*Richard S. Westfall*
6.	**Elizabeth I**	*Patrick Collinson*
7.	**George III**	*John Cannon*
8.	**Benjamin Disraeli**	*Jonathan Parry*
9.	**Christopher Wren**	*Kerry Downes*
10.	**John Ruskin**	*Robert Hewison*
11.	**James Joyce**	*Bruce Stewart*
12.	**John Milton**	*Gordon Campbell*
13.	**Jane Austen**	*Marilyn Butler*
14.	**Henry VIII**	*Eric Ives*
15.	**Queen Victoria**	*K. D. Reynolds and H. C. G. Matthew*
16.	**Winston Churchill**	*Paul Addison*
17.	**Oliver Cromwell**	*John Morrill*
18.	**Thomas Paine**	*Mark Philp*
19.	**J. M. W. Turner**	*Luke Herrmann*
20.	**William and Mary**	*Tony Claydon and W. A. Speck*

Oliver Cromwell

VIP

Very Interesting People

John Morrill

OXFORD
UNIVERSITY PRESS

OXFORD
UNIVERSITY PRESS

Great Clarendon Street, Oxford ox2 6DP

Oxford University Press is a department of the University of Oxford.
It furthers the University's objective of excellence in research, scholarship,
and education by publishing worldwide in

Oxford New York

Auckland Cape Town Dar es Salaam Hong Kong Karachi
Kuala Lumpur Madrid Melbourne Mexico City Nairobi
New Delhi Shanghai Taipei Toronto

With offices in

Argentina Austria Brazil Chile Czech Republic France Greece
Guatemala Hungary Italy Japan Poland Portugal Singapore
South Korea Switzerland Thailand Turkey Ukraine Vietnam

Oxford is a registered trade mark of Oxford University Press
in the UK and in certain other countries

Published in the United States
by Oxford University Press Inc., New York

First published in the *Oxford Dictionary of National Biography* 2004
This paperback edition first published 2007

First published 2007

British Library Cataloguing in Publication Data

Data available

Library of Congress Cataloging in Publication Data

Data available

Typeset by SPI Publisher Services, Pondicherry, India
Printed in Great Britain
on acid-free paper by
Clays Ltd, St Ives plc

ISBN 978-0-19-953450-0

1

For David Smith

Friend and colleague for a quarter of a century

Contents

Preface

I have been living with Oliver Cromwell for more than forty years. I first thought about him historically when I was in my last two years at school, taught by Norman Dore, a miner's son from South Wales who looked uncannily like him—he even had warts on his face, though not in quite the right places! I wrote the best essay of my undergraduate years about him (for Keith Thomas). Cromwell had a walk-on part in my doctoral thesis, for the hero of my story—the Cheshire puritan-parliamentarian soldier and politician, William Brereton (another man strangely exempted from the Self-Denying Ordinance)—collaborated with him up to, but not really beyond, the regicide. My early writings all circled round him, but I was inexorably drawn into closer and closer study of his letters and speeches. I suppose the key moment was an invitation to be president of the Cromwell Association in 1989, a position I proudly held for a decade. Over the years I have given well over 100 talks about him in schools, branches of the Historical Association, universities, and conferences. I have in fact spoken about him on all five continents, including at a Jesuit university, a Seventh-Day

Adventist college, and at Drogheda. I have been physically attacked (with a furled umbrella) and received hate mail. The invitation to sum up all that I had learned here, in this pithy life, originally commissioned for the *Oxford Dictionary of National Biography* (2004), seemed the perfect opportunity to bring it all together.

I am a Roman Catholic deacon, and I had my own conversion experience in Holy Week 1977, pretty much 350 years after the conversion experience Cromwell describes in one of his letters (quoted from in chapter one of this book). Because we share a conversion experience, there are important ways in which I understand him. Because he is a seventeenth-century puritan, there are equally important ways in which there is a great divide between us. What I admire about him is his constant striving to put his faith into practice, to submit himself to the will of God; what alarms me about him is the self-righteousness which allowed him to judge others. But then again his willingness to look beyond outward form and observances to the inner man (or woman, but then he was very much a man's man), his ability to discern 'the root of the matter' in 'all species of Christian' attracts, just as his willingness to let God's ends justify brutal humans means repels. 'Cruel necessity', he is reported to have said, as he looked down on Charles I's corpse in its coffin after the regicide; here necessity is a word linked to providence—God's will must be done even when it seems cruel in human eyes. So—to the incredulity of the bishop who ordained me—I can be a Catholic and an admirer of a man who had both greatness and warts on the inside, as well as on the outside.

It would have been a lot easier to write a 100,000-word life of Oliver than one of 30,000, as originally requested for the *Oxford DNB*. This is a distillation of years of reflection on all Cromwell's surviving words (some half a million of them), and the words of those who knew him and—by and large—distrusted him. I wish to thank the 100 or so students at Cambridge who took my 'special subject' course across the six years straddling the 400th anniversary of Cromwell's birth (and the 350th of the regicide). I want to thank Frank Bremer with whom I taught two hugely enjoyable summer schools on Cromwell and the colonial governor John Winthrop ('two faces of puritanism'), especially for his scepticism. I have learnt so much from colleagues with whom I have debated over beer and whisk(e)y, most obviously Colin Davis and Blair Worden. Above all I want to thank all those graduate students of mine who have wrestled with Cromwell—especially Tim Wales and Andrew Barclay who shared with me their recoveries of material which has transformed their and my understanding of his early life. Among all these former pupils, colleagues, and friends, I want to thank David L. Smith, who is all those things to me, above all a true friend. I would like to dedicate this book to him, with gratitude.

John Morrill
Candlemas 2007

About the author

John Morrill is Professor of British and Irish History at the University of Cambridge and a Fellow of Selwyn College. He was Consultant Editor for all the seventeenth-century lives in the *Oxford Dictionary of National Biography*. He is the author and editor of twenty books mainly about the seventeenth century, including *The Oxford Illustrated History of Tudor and Stuart Britain* (1996) and *Oliver Cromwell and the English Revolution* (1990). He continues to explore aspects of Cromwell's thought and career, and recent essays include 'The Cromwellian context of the Drogheda massacre' and 'How Oliver Cromwell thought'. Cromwell also played a prominent part in his 2006 Ford Lectures at Oxford, entitled *Living with Revolution* which will be published shortly.

Rising from obscurity, 1599–1642

1

Oliver Cromwell (1599–1658),

lord protector of England, Scotland, and Ireland, was the second son of Robert Cromwell (*d.* 1617) and his wife, Elizabeth Steward (*d.* 1654); he was born in Huntingdon on 25 April 1599 and was baptized in St John's Church there four days later. He was named after his father's elder brother, Sir Oliver Cromwell of Hinchingbrooke and of Ramsey, who almost certainly stood as his godfather.

Early life and marriage

The Cromwell fortune and name derived from Cromwell's great-grandfather, Morgan Williams, a Welshman from Glamorgan who had settled in Putney as an innkeeper and brewer and who had had the good fortune to marry the elder sister of Henry VIII's great minister Thomas Cromwell before the latter's rise to greatness. Williams and his son Richard were beneficiaries of this relationship and received enough confiscated church lands to become one of the most prominent families in Huntingdonshire. In slightly defiant gratitude (Thomas Cromwell having been beheaded in 1540) Richard changed his family name to Cromwell. Conscious of the circumstances, Oliver, throughout his life and even as lord protector, occasionally described himself as Williams alias Cromwell. Richard's son Sir Henry Cromwell ('the golden knight', 1536–1604) built substantial houses on the sites of a dissolved Benedictine convent (Hinchingbrooke, half a mile from Huntingdon) and a dissolved Benedictine abbey (Ramsey, 15 miles away in the fenland). Sir Oliver (1563–1655), uncle and godfather of the future lord protector, thus inherited a large but debt-laden estate (debt made worse by over-frequent receptions of members of the royal family as they travelled up the Great North Road, less than a mile away). Cromwell's father in contrast inherited a modest cluster of urban properties and impropriations in and around Huntingdon, but no manors or freehold land. With an income of perhaps £300 per annum and a seven-room town house, Robert Cromwell was a substantial inhabitant of a secondary town. He represented it in the parliament of 1593. None the less, as the eldest (surviving) son of the younger son of a knight Cromwell's social status was ambiguous.

Oliver Cromwell's mother was the daughter of William Steward. William's father in the early days of the Reformation had secured from his own brother, as prior of Ely, long leases of abbey (later dean and chapter) lands. Those leases passed to Elizabeth's childless brother Thomas, and eventually to Oliver.

Very little is known about Cromwell's first forty years. Only four of his personal letters survive, together with the précis of a speech he made when the House of Commons was in grand committee in 1628. He made only fleeting and impersonal appearances in public records. During his first decade there is the record of his baptism and of his having been a boy at the town grammar school, sitting at the feet of Thomas Beard, a pluralist and rather complacent conformist, whose reputation rested principally on his having written a best-seller on the way God visited divine justice in this world on scandalous sinners. There is a story that when the future Charles I, aged three, stayed at Hinchingbrooke on his way south to join his father, Sir Henry brought his four-year-old grandson Oliver to play with him; and that they squabbled and Oliver punched the prince on the nose and made it bleed. The story was recorded only after Oliver had orchestrated Charles's death, and it seems just too good to be true.

During Cromwell's second decade there is the record of his matriculation at Sidney Sussex College, Cambridge, on 23 April 1616 and of his departure from the college on 24 June 1617, immediately after the death of his father. Some early biographers claimed that he then attended Lincoln's Inn, but there is no trace of him in its records and no evidence of a common-law training in his later discourse. With a widowed mother and seven unmarried sisters the eighteen-year-old Oliver is more likely to have returned home. The next ten years would have necessarily been spent in coping with being the only man in a household of women. In effect, it meant trying to find husbands for his sisters who would be worthy of family honour and not ask for too much by way of dowry. Since his mother did not marry again and lived on as a widow until 1654, this was a major drain on the attenuated family fortune.

During Cromwell's third decade (April 1619 to April 1629) there is slightly more evidence. His marriage on 22 August 1620 is recorded in the registers of St Giles Cripplegate, London, as is his return in at least some of the annual elections to the common council of Huntingdon (the records are too incomplete for greater precision about how often). The subsidy rolls for the mid-1620s place him among the top twenty householders in the town. A brief and secular letter in 1626 to Henry Downhall—an old university friend, now a minister with Arminian leanings—inviting him to stand as godfather to Richard, his third son, suggests that Oliver's puritan conversion lay before him. In 1627 his uncle Oliver, who had massive debts, sold Hinchingbrooke to Sidney Montagu, brother of the first earl of Manchester and, like him, a thrusting lawyer with court aspirations, and retreated to the family's larger house at Ramsey. Initially this led to a new honour for Cromwell, as he was selected in 1628 to represent in parliament the borough of Huntingdon as junior member behind a scion of the Montagus. He made virtually no impact on the very full records of that parliament except for one gauche speech, which fell like a stone, against the Arminian, Bishop Richard Neile.

The crucial event of this decade was his marriage to Elizabeth Bourchier (1598–1665). She was the eldest of twelve children of Sir James Bourchier, a retired London fur trader with extensive land in Essex (and elsewhere) and with strong connections with the godly gentry families there. The marriage was probably arranged by Oliver's father's sister Joan, wife of Sir Francis Barrington, who certainly brokered many other family matches. It brought Oliver into contact with the Barringtons, the Mashams, and the St Johns and also with leading members of the London merchant community, and behind them all the great interest of the Rich family, headed by the earls of Warwick and Holland. Cromwell's marriage was to be long and stable. There were nine children: five boys and four girls. One son (James) died as an infant (1632), and two others on the eve of manhood—the eldest, Robert (1622–1639), while away at school and the second, Oliver (1623–1644), of camp fever while serving as a parliamentarian officer. But two sons—Richard Cromwell (1626–1712) and Henry Cromwell (1628–1674)—and four daughters—Bridget (*bap.* 1624, *d.* 1662), Elizabeth (*bap.* 1629, *d.* 1658), Mary (*bap.* 1637, *d.* 1713), and Frances (*bap.* 1638, *d.* 1720)—played their part in the great affairs of the 1650s. Little is known of the relationship between Oliver and Elizabeth beyond the unmannered deep affection of their letters to one another in the early 1650s and her apparent utter loyalty and discreet public presence on state occasions under the protectorate.

Crisis and recovery

There is evidence that Cromwell was suffering from physical and mental stress by 1628. He took the waters at Wellingborough for severe stomach cramps, and the papers of Sir Theodore Turquet de Mayerne, a London doctor, record his seeking treatment on 19 September 1628 for *valde melancolicus* (depression). According to a much later report, in 1628 or 1629 he experienced the religious conversion which henceforth dominated his life and was recorded graphically in a letter of 1638 to his cousin. Following on from this he became involved in a number of confrontations, all of which he lost. He became embroiled in a local feud that is chronicled in the records of the Mercers' Company over several years from 1628. The Mercers were trustees of a bequest left for the benefit of Huntingdon by a member of the company, Richard Fishbourne, who had been born in the town. Cromwell can be found lobbying for the money to be used not to underwrite an existing lectureship held by his old conformist schoolmaster Thomas Beard but a new one to be held by a firebrand puritan, Robert Procter. Then in 1630 the Montagus procured a new charter for Huntingdon, and replaced the council elected annually by the freemen with a closed oligarchy, from which Cromwell was excluded. His public accusations of malpractice against the Montagus and their lawyer led to his being called before the privy council in December 1630 and forced to admit his error. On 7 May 1631 Cromwell (and his mother and his wife) entered into a deed of sale of almost all their properties in and around Huntingdon for the sum of £1800, which suggests an annual value of about £100. Oliver, Elizabeth, and the children moved to a farmstead in St Ives, 4 miles away. For the next five years he may have remained a gentleman by birth but he was a plain russet-coated yeoman by lifestyle.

The next few years are no less murky than the previous ones. Yet the silence of the records about Cromwell is itself striking. There is no suggestion that he was ever presented before the church courts for any form of recusancy or non-conformity, and cryptic (but unexplained) memoranda in the papers of Matthew Wren, the Laudian bishop of Ely, for November and December 1638 and March 1640 suggest that he was using Cromwell in helping to resolve a number of disputes. Cromwell was not included in any sheriffs' list for non-payment or obstruction of ship money, nor was he reported to the council for any more ill-advised words. In 1637 he is reported to have offered legal advice to commoners in the Isle of Ely whose livelihoods were threatened by the drainage of the fens, but there is no shred of evidence that he opposed the principle of the land improvement, let alone that he condoned riot or extra-legal protest against it.

From 1631 to 1636 Cromwell lived and worked as a farmer in St Ives, suffering from an intractable chest infection that led him to wear a red flannel around his throat, even to church. Perhaps his move stemmed from an accumulation of debt from having too many sisters to marry off, compounded by having lost status, honour, and such authority as he had possessed in Huntingdon. But there is another intriguing possibility: when he moved to St Ives in 1631 he became a tenant of the godly Henry Lawrence, just after Lawrence had become one of the ten patentees of Connecticut in New England, and had committed himself to moving to this colony as soon as he could; Cromwell's selling up and moving when he did could well indicate his intention to move there with him. In 1634 Lawrence and his co-patentees wrote to John Winthrop, the governor of Massachusetts, and announced their imminent departure from England. But they never arrived, either because Winthrop would not meet their preconditions, or because the privy council prevented this particular group from travelling. This is the allegation that several later royalists and the New England minister Cotton Mather later made with respect to Cromwell himself and others. In the event, Lawrence went instead to Arnhem in the Netherlands, where he became a noted lay preacher and wrote against paedobaptism. Perhaps he was becoming too radical for New England. There may have been many reasons why Cromwell did not go with him, but one is almost certainly the happenstance that in January 1636, just as Lawrence was emigrating, Oliver's childless and widowed maternal uncle Sir Thomas Steward died. Cromwell—who may have been spending time securing a court order to protect his inheritance by having the old man declared a lunatic (probably because senility was advancing)—inherited from him leases on tithes held by the dean and chapter of Ely, and he and his family moved to a substantial glebe house in the shadow of the cathedral. His income increased dramatically to some £300 a year. The tide had turned.

Puritanism and parliament

In addition, there are tantalizing hints in two letters written in 1636 and 1638 that Cromwell had established himself within an East Anglian puritan network emanating from his extended family. On 11 January 1636 Cromwell wrote to a London mercer, George Storie. He reminded Storie (who, he did not realize, had just migrated to New England) that he was late with his subscription for a lectureship in Godmanchester, which abuts Huntingdon but lies across the River Ouse in a different diocese; the lectureship had been set up after the failure of the godly to secure the Fishbourne bequest in 1629. The peremptory tone of a working farmer to a rich London merchant is startling. In an age where recognizing relative social status mattered, this was an inappropriate letter, unless Cromwell was writing on behalf of a group which included Storie's betters. Furthermore, in prompting Storie to pay up, Cromwell spoke of the need for such lectureship posts 'in these times wherein they are suppressed with too much haste and violence by the enemies of God his truth', clearly a snarling reference to the bishops (*Letters and Speeches*, 1904, letter 1).

A second letter, written on 13 October 1638, is much stronger evidence of a fierce puritan faith. It is addressed to his 22-year-old cousin Elizabeth, the young bride of Oliver St John (*c*.1598–1673), Cromwell's exact contemporary at Cambridge and principal attorney to Cromwell's cousin John Hampden in the ship-money trial just concluded. It is a passionate account of how after having been 'a chief, the chief of sinners', driven to the depths of despair, he had been called to be among 'the congregation of the firstborn [the firstborn son of God, Christ]' so that 'my body rests in hope, and if here I may serve my God either by my doing or by my suffering, I shall be most glad' (*Letters and Speeches*, 1904, letter 2). His religious journey had begun before 1630 but it is possible that he had been further radicalized by Job Tookey, the curate of St Ives, hounded out by Bishop John Williams of Lincoln in 1635. His link to Lawrence also makes plausible a claim made in a report in other respects very accurate that by the later 1630s Cromwell regularly preached in other men's houses as well as in his own.

By the end of 1639, then, Cromwell was a radicalized puritan with powerful links through the families of his father and of his wife to leading puritan families in Essex and London and to some of the leading figures who had emigrated to New England, including Robert Hooke, whose marriage had been arranged by Joan, Lady Barrington, the aunt who had probably arranged his own wedding. Cromwell's personal fortunes—and his health—had waned in the 1620s, reached a low plateau in the early 1630s, and had waxed in the later 1630s. Providence had smiled on him. If in the years in and immediately after his conversion he had served God by his suffering, he was about to find out how he could serve him by his doing.

If Cromwell had died in his fortieth year he would have made no mark on history, and would be unknown except to the antiquaries of Huntingdonshire. Yet from this lowly position he was to emerge as the most powerful figure in revolutionary times, and this made him loved and reviled in equal measure. He was in his own day, and has remained ever since, one of the most contended of Englishmen. He was a man born on the cusp of the gentry and the middling sort who became a head of state. He was a general whose brutal conquests of Scotland and (particularly) Ireland have cast a long dark shadow. He was a king-killer who agonized about whether to be king; a parliamentarian who used military force to break and to purge parliaments. He was a passionate advocate of religious liberty who stood by and let books be burnt and blasphemers be publicly tortured. He was an advocate of equitable justice who imprisoned not only those who challenged his powers to raise extra-parliamentary taxation but also the lawyers who had the temerity to represent them. To his admirers he overthrew tyranny and strove to promote liberty. To his detractors he was an ambitious hypocrite who betrayed the cause of liberty he claimed to represent. And it all began with his very surprising return to the parliaments of 1640 as MP for the city of Cambridge.

Cromwell must have been the least wealthy man returned to both the Short and the Long parliaments, and he was returned for a borough that had always returned a prominent client of the lord keeper and a prominent resident of the borough. Only one existing account makes any sense of his selection. An anonymous report, integrated into the wholly scurrilous and unreliable *Flagellum* after the death of the first compiler, James Heath, is full of verifiable detail. It tells how a group of godly freemen, headed by the mayor's brother-in-law (who, like Cromwell, held a tenancy in St Ives) and inspired by Cromwell's 'preaching' at a conventicle, persuaded the mayor on 7 January 1640 to make Cromwell a freeman on the mayor's own nomination. This made him eligible to stand for election as MP for Cambridge, and the same group subsequently pressed his cause, securing his return in March 1640 in second place behind the lord keeper's nominee and in October in first place ahead of a prominent puritan common-councilman to the exclusion of the court candidate. Less reliable, but also quite possible, is a later memoir that claimed that when in September 1640 a group of twelve opposition peers refused to obey Charles I's summons to York, Oliver St John brought Cromwell into the small group that helped to draft the peers' petition and to carry it to the north.

This trajectory—a well-connected man with passionate views about the way that the godly were being driven out of the church or persecuted if they sought to witness within it—helps to explain the prominent part Cromwell played in the early months of the Long Parliament. It would explain how he came to be trusted with responsibility in the very first week for presenting the petition of one of the great puritan martyrs of Star Chamber, John Lilburne, for securing his release from prison and the promise of compensation for his savage flogging. It would explain how he came to be the man who in May 1641 moved the second reading of the Annual Parliaments Bill, and how soon afterwards he came to take so leading a part in drafting the bill for the suspension of episcopacy. In those opening months he served on eighteen high-profile committees, especially those concerned with investigating religious innovation and abuse of ecclesiastical power. His faith and trust in God made him fearless. And more than once he spoke his mind too forcefully and was reproved by the house (as in his unvarnished attack on episcopacy in February 1641). Sir Philip Warwick memorably recalled him as wearing a plain cloth suit, and plain linen shirt, its collar spotted with blood. It is an image of a man short of a change of clothes and without a servant to shave him: a man on the margins socially and not entirely at ease with himself. As a result he was dropped from the opposition front bench speaker's panel after May 1641. He remained a useful man on committees, pushing for religious reform and a strong line against the Irish rebels. But as time went on he spoke less in the full house.

The first civil war, 1642–1645

2

Parliamentary strong man in East Anglia

In the high summer of 1642 king and parliament were increasingly provoking one another into trial by battle. The Rubicon was finally crossed when Charles I raised his standard at Nottingham on 22 August. He had written on 25 July to the vice-chancellor of Cambridge University inviting the colleges to assist him by the 'loan' of their plate. Cromwell was sent down by the Commons to prevent them from doing so. On 10 August, accompanied by perhaps 200 lightly armed countrymen who had volunteered to help him, he blocked the exit road from Cambridge that led to the Great North Road. He went on to intimidate his way into Cambridge Castle and to seize the arms stored there, and halt the movement of silver. At a time when most Englishmen were dithering and waiting upon events, it was a bold and unhesitating act. Within a fortnight he had raised a company of sixty cavalry, recruiting his cousin Edward Whalley and his brother-in-law John Disbrowe to be his lieutenants, and he used his troopers to search the houses of suspected royalists. In mid-October he was instructed to take his troop to join the army assembled by the earl of Essex, the captain-general of the parliamentarian forces; he arrived at some point during the battle of Edgehill and may have taken some part in its end-game. He remained with the earl until 13 November at Turnham Green (5 miles west of London): the stand-off there caused the king to abandon his attempt to enter his capital and to withdraw first to Reading and then to Oxford. Cromwell's movements for the rest of the year are unknown, but a return to Ely and to organizing the defence of the area seems likelier than a return to the House of Commons. Certainly from 6 January to 13 March 1643 he was in Cambridgeshire and west Suffolk.

In the course of February 1643, without being in more than the odd skirmish, Cromwell was inexplicably promoted from captain to colonel. Parliament had appointed William Grey, Lord Grey of Warke, as major-general of the forces for the defence of the six eastern counties, and Cromwell's appointment was to one of the regiments Grey now sought to raise. But the appointment quickly took on a greater significance because on 7 April Grey took the great bulk of his force, some 5000 men, and set off to join the earl of Essex at the siege of Reading. He never returned. For the rest of 1643 Cromwell was effectively the senior officer in the six parliamentarian heartland counties of East Anglia: Essex, Hertfordshire, Huntingdonshire, Cambridgeshire, Suffolk, and Norfolk. He had no experience as a militia captain, let alone as a deputy lieutenant—he had learned nothing of war from his father, his grandfather, his uncles. He was a gentleman by birth but he was not the equal of any of the men who ran the county committees or the lieutenancies of the six associated counties. Yet from the outset he, and he alone, seems to have formed a strategic plan for the defence of the region with the fierce insistence of a sergeant-major dealing with a bunch of officer cadets who had yet to realize that war was a life-and-death matter: 'you must act lively; do it without distraction. Neglect no means' (*Letters and Speeches*, 1904, letter 14, 6 August 1643); 'Service must be done. Command you and be obeyed!'—this in a letter endorsed, 'to the deputy-lieutenants of Essex: these, haste, haste, posthaste' (ibid., 3.316, 6 August 1643).

In a sense, Cromwell's task was simple: there was no threat from the east (the sea), from the south, or from the west. But there were all kinds of pockets of anti-parliamentarian sentiment within the region, and there was a threat that grew steadily throughout the spring and summer from the north as the royalist army of the earl of Newcastle inexorably took control of Lincolnshire and of the Great North Road as far south as Stamford. With no more than 2000 men to hand at any one time, Cromwell had reason to be fearful.

Cromwell had three priorities. His first was to act decisively and firmly to deal with any royalist stirs (hence his rapid march and seizure of Lowestoft on 13–14 March 1643 and King's Lynn the following week). His second was to secure and defend all the bridges and routes across first the Great Ouse and then the Nene (which involved the bombardment and occupation of small royalist outposts like Crowland and Burghley House). It is astounding that he could write with such confidence in June that 'two or three hundred men in these parts are enough' (*Calendar of the Wynn (of Gwydir) Papers, 1515–1690*, 1926, no. 1722A [p. 280]), a judgement borne out by the fact that a royalist regiment under Colonel

Sir John Palgrave was repulsed by the small garrison he had left in Peterborough. No one else was attempting to do anything. By his own strenuous efforts and intuitive strategic sense Cromwell secured East Anglia for the parliament. The coping stone to this effort was the establishment of military headquarters for the region at Ely and his own appointment as governor of the Isle of Ely. This was achieved in July 1643.

Cromwell's third priority was to establish an effective supply system to ensure a steady flow of new soldiers and of regular pay and provisions. That meant galvanizing the various county committees, each of which was more concerned with its own defence than with the defence of the wider region. In addition, each county found itself more focused on sending money off to Lord Grey's brigade serving with the earl of Essex than on supplying Master Cromwell's troopers. As the latter's sense of military achievement grew, so did his self-confidence. His pleading turned to peremptory command. And the staccato notes began to have an effect.

The most striking aspect of Cromwell's letters from the summer of 1643 was his insistence that no religious test be applied to those volunteering for service. He needed more men, and the more committed to the cause the better. He later recalled advising John Hampden that a reliance of 'old decayed serving men and tapsters' would not secure victory; rather he called on him to 'get men of a spirit ... that is like to go as far as a gentleman will go, or else I am sure you will be beaten still' (*Speeches*, 134, 13 April 1657). His most famous statement in this respect is that 'I had rather have a plain russet-coated captain that knows what he fights for, and loves what he knows, than that which you call a gentleman and is nothing else. I honour a gentleman that is so indeed' (*Letters and Speeches*, 1904, letter 16, 11 September 1643). Better a godly commoner than an inactive gentleman, for sure; but better a committed commoner than a committed gentleman? That is not so clear. If, as seems possible, in the lost original Cromwell wrote 'I honour a gentleman who is so in deed' rather than 'indeed', the social animus is stronger—he will honour only a gentleman who is fully active in the cause. And then there are the implications of his statement that 'if you choose honest men to be captains of horse, honest men will follow them, and they will be careful to mount such' (ibid.). If gentlemen are followed by their retainers, then honest men are followed by honest men. But the 'honest man' he had in mind was Ralph Margery, a farmer from Walsham-le-Willows, Suffolk. Margery and his wife had been outspoken and principled puritan nonconformists in the 1630s, and Margery was an unreconciled excommunicate from 1638 onwards. He was quick to volunteer once the war started and had gained notoriety for exceeding orders in the arbitrary seizure of horses from suspected royalists. Both his religious enthusiasm and this freedom in implementing orders against delinquents made the county committee distrust him. Twice Cromwell commanded the Suffolk committee to confirm his appointment and look for more like him. As Newcastle's army came ever closer, Cromwell's insistence became ever more shrill.

Having thus created a strong defensive line across the southern fenland, radiating out from Ely, Cromwell offered his services to the beleaguered forces to the north, and he made a number of sallies from his redoubt to help to push back royalist probes. Twice he joined up with an improvised body of troops from other counties—once at Sleaford, Lincolnshire, early in May 1643, and once at Nottingham early in June, with a view to a concerted advance into royalist areas, but each time the mission was aborted. A sweep through Lincolnshire in July did culminate in a stiff skirmish at Gainsborough on the 27th, Cromwell's first real experience of what it was to lead a cavalry charge and maintain discipline through and after the charge. The ability to regroup victorious cavalry and to redirect them against other opponents, so crucial to his part in the victories of Marston Moor and Naseby, was learned at Gainsborough. Much of the summer was spent either at regional headquarters in Cambridgeshire or in strengthening Lincolnshire against the royalists, culminating in another important (though rash) cavalry charge at Winceby as, in conjunction with Yorkshire forces under Sir Thomas Fairfax, he routed a significant royalist force sent out from Newark. After this battle Cromwell came to be known in the royalist press as 'the Lord of the Fens' (*Mercurius Aulicus*, 4–11 November 1643).

The victorious captain

Grey's secondment to Essex's army, the lack of co-ordination within the six East Anglian counties, and the threat posed by Newcastle's advances caused parliament to rethink its policies for the region. Early in August Edward Montagu, second earl of Manchester, was given military command over the eastern association, a much stronger and more centralized committee system was established, and conscription was introduced (this is a context for some of Cromwell's tough letters about the need for more russet-coated captains and honest men). Cromwell was initially just one of the many colonels appointed by Manchester as he struggled to raise an army of 14,000 men, but from the beginning he was in *de facto* command of the cavalry, and this was formalized in February 1644 when he was appointed lieutenant-general of Manchester's army. Throughout the winter of 1643–4 he was busy in and around Cambridge and in the counties to the west (as far as Northampton), although this involved little military action. The entry of the Scots into the war caused the marquess of Newcastle to look north and this relieved pressure on Lincolnshire and therefore on the association. Cromwell—working closely with Manchester—was released to assist the parliamentarian war effort first in Yorkshire and then in the midlands. Cromwell thus felt able to return briefly to parliament (mid-January to mid-February 1644), long enough to bring a series of charges against Lord Willoughby of Parham for the inefficiency and mismanagement of the defence of Lincolnshire, resulting in Willoughby's resignation and the extension of Manchester's commission to cover that county. Cromwell then, belatedly, took the solemn league and covenant and was immediately appointed a member of the committee of both kingdoms which had been charged with managing the whole strategy of war and peace. He was clearly recognized as a rising man.

Cromwell continued to seek out those most committed to the cause, and that certainly did include dedicated presbyterians as well as sectaries. In January 1644 he supported the energetic presbyterian Edward King for promotion in Lincolnshire, and twice he dissuaded Lieutenant-Colonel William Dodson from resigning in protest at having to serve with sectaries. But this goodwill was not reciprocated. In

March 1644 Lawrence Crawford, the Scottish major-general responsible for the infantry in Manchester's army, sought for good reason to dismiss William Packer, a Baptist junior officer, and engaged in heated exchanges with Cromwell over it. Initially Manchester stood aloof from these disputes, being a man temperamentally both drawn to a reformed Erastian episcopal settlement and willing to commission and support William Dowsing as his agent for systematic orderly iconoclasm across Suffolk and Cambridgeshire. But eventually he came to side with Crawford.

Late in February 1644 Cromwell returned to his command and set out to expand the frontiers of the parliamentarian eastern redoubt: he took Hillesdon House (Buckinghamshire) on 9 March, and was involved both in the storm of Lincoln (6 May) and in the repulse of George Goring's attempt to relieve the town. Manchester and Cromwell then joined up with the northern army under the Fairfaxes and the Scots to take York. In response the king's principal marching army headed north to combine with the marquess of Newcastle to relieve the town.

That in due course led to the greatest of all civil-war battles, at Marston Moor on 2 July 1644. Cromwell's role in that battle remains contentious. He commanded the left wing of the allied army, consisting of his own eastern cavalry and three regiments of Scots cavalry. Cromwell himself received a nasty flesh wound in the neck early on and needed treatment, but he returned in time to take responsibility for the final, decisive charge. The official English reports gave all the praise to Cromwell and none to the Scots—Cromwell himself, in a private letter, spoke only of 'a few Scots in the rear' (*Letters and Speeches*, 1904, letter 21, 5 July 1644)—and David Leslie, who commanded the wing in his absence and whose regiments were crucial to disrupting the royalist centre, and his fellow Scots took great umbrage. That the London press should henceforth call Cromwell 'Ironside' and in due course his troops the Ironsides, in recognition of his victory, rubbed salt into the wound. Cromwell himself neither claimed nor disclaimed responsibility for the victory; he ascribed it entirely to God. In a moving letter to his brother-in-law Valentine Walton, breaking to him the news of the agonizing death from a shattered and amputated leg of Valentine's oldest son, Cromwell spoke of it as 'an absolute victory obtained by the Lord's blessing upon the godly party principally ... Give glory, all the glory, to God'. And, in one of his most memorable metaphors, he wrote that 'God made them as stubble to our swords' (ibid., letter 21, 5 July 1644). The process by which he came to see himself and his cause as peculiarly blessed by God was well in train. Cromwell had no doubt that he was no longer serving God by his suffering but by his doing, and he was most glad.

The New Model Army

Those who served over and alongside Cromwell failed to exploit the victory. For two months Manchester dallied over the siege of Doncaster, and he then unhurriedly moved back into the eastern association. By now the tensions and resentments both over the composition of the army and the need to help out wherever the cause was under pressure had become seriously debilitating, and Crawford and Cromwell went up to London and presented their alternative accounts of their relationship one with another. Each sought the dismissal of the other, and each had too much political support to be sacked. The Commons established a committee to 'consider the means of uniting presbyterians and Independents', which was a startling admission of the scale of the problem. But their stated willingness to 'endeavour of finding out some way how far tender consciences... may be borne with' was a considerable concession to Cromwell's position (*Journals of the House of Commons*, 3, 1642–4, 626). Manchester broke the deadlock by calling on both parties to unite in common service but they returned to their military duties deeply antagonized.

In the spirit of the uneasy concord Manchester and Cromwell began the process of squeezing the royalist headquarters at Oxford by taking out its satellite garrisons in Oxfordshire, Berkshire, and Northamptonshire. Then, as the king returned from his triumph over the earl of Essex in Cornwall, Manchester joined Sir William Waller's army of the southern association to block his passage at Newbury. The result was an unsatisfactorily drawn battle in which Cromwell unaccountably delayed engaging his cavalry until it was too late to make an overall victory possible. He then sulked for two days and failed to carry out a direct order from Manchester to prevent the king from relieving and securing Donnington Castle. He also took part in a council of war in which he was scathing about Manchester's failings. Relations between the two men were beyond repair and, within a month, on and after 23 November both were back at Westminster hell-bent on destroying each other.

The feud between Manchester and Cromwell was symptomatic of parliamentarianism in almost every region—and if not every major-general had recalcitrant subordinates, most of them were unwilling to take orders from or show respect to the captain-general himself. The earl of Essex, stranded and cut off in Cornwall, was forced into an abject surrender at Lostwithiel that brought disgrace upon his head. It was therefore in the interests of his friends to spread the responsibility for the failures of the cause since Marston Moor as widely as possible. His friends laid the blame for the failure of the Newbury campaign on those who put godly enthusiasm ahead of 'wisdom and valour'. Godliness versus aristocratic prudence was now the crunch issue. Stung by public and private criticism which seemed more directed at them than at Manchester, Waller and Cromwell decided to take the initiative. On 25 November they reported to the Commons that all the failings of the past three months resulted from Manchester's inability or unwillingness to take decisive action at the right time. Perhaps Cromwell expected Manchester to roll over as Willoughby had done in January. But there was nothing indecisive or lacklustre in Manchester's response. On 28 November he rebutted the charges of incompetence, implicating Waller and Cromwell in all the mistaken decisions, and accusing them of failing to carry out direct orders to the detriment of the cause. He then accused Cromwell in particular of vilifying the Westminster assembly, displaying a violent animosity towards the Scots, and being opposed in principle to the hereditary peerage. Each house now set up a committee to investigate the claims of its own member. Meanwhile Essex convened a meeting of his own friends, of Manchester's allies, and of the Scots, to see if under the terms of the solemn league and covenant the Scots could impeach Cromwell as an incendiary.

As the temperature rose and mutual recrimination mounted, some men remembered there was a common enemy who hoped to see their heads on spikes or their bodies dangling from ropes. God would not bless a cause so divided, nor give victory to men who had failed to honour him consistently. 'The chief causes of division are pride and covetousness', the presbyterian Zouch Tate told the house (*Writings and Speeches*, 1.314). Let all those who had held commissions surrender them; let all MPs return to Westminster and let there be a fresh start. Cromwell was quick to accept the proposition. Over the next four months the principles of self-denial and of the rationalization of the armies operating in the areas firmly under parliamentarian control (viz., the armies of Essex, Manchester, and Waller) were rarely questioned. Who was to decide on a new command structure, and whether, and if so in whose favour, exceptions to the principle of self-denial were to be made, became and remained bitterly divisive questions. It is possible that Cromwell was privy to, and ready to promote, the self-denying ordinance; it is unlikely (but not impossible) that he hoped and planned to be excepted from its operation. When he said that he hoped 'no Members of either House will scruple to deny themselves, and their own private interests, for the public good' (ibid., 1.314–15) he was probably speaking from the heart. There can be no doubt that he was one of those who prevented Essex from being excepted, and one of those who strenuously supported Sir Thomas Fairfax's elevation to command the New Model Army; but his own exemption was never fully approved by both houses, and seemed against the odds until after Prince Rupert's sack of Leicester on 30 May 1645 threatened a major escalation of the war. When the struggle over the list of officers was being fought out within and between the houses Cromwell was away, serving under Waller. Waller later recalled that Cromwell was blunt in his manner, but that he did not bear himself with any pride or disdain, and that he had never disputed Waller's orders. In the event the failure of the two houses to agree on a lieutenant-general led on 3 April and 12 May to Cromwell's being granted two forty-day appointments. As the second came to an end Fairfax moved, at a council of war on 13 June 1645, that Cromwell be appointed for the duration of the war. The Lords would not agree to it and in the event his commission was renewed for periods of three, four, and finally six months, so that he remained in the army until mid-July 1646. No other MP was exempted from the self-denying ordinance to serve in the New Model Army, although two provincial commanders were given similar temporary extensions. By early 1646 many New Model officers were securing positions in the Commons as a result of the 'recruiter elections' by which the places of secluded royalists were filled via by-elections. Cromwell was not the sole MP in the army for long.

Cromwell's part in the victories of the New Model Army in the last eighteen months of the war was striking. His role at the battle of Naseby (14 June 1645) in driving half the royalist cavalry from the field and regrouping to break the discipline and will of the royalist infantry was pivotal. His role at Langport (10 July), where his own troopers stormed a narrow ford in the face of concentrated enemy fire with complete self-belief and passion, demonstrates that their faith in Cromwell was as great as his faith in God. He then took part in the sieges of Bridgwater, Sherborne, Bristol, Devizes, and Winchester; and, with Fairfax, he succeeded in brushing aside 20,000 Clubmen on the Dorset/Wiltshire border. This relentless phase culminated in the brutal assault, destruction, and pillaging of the Catholic marquess of Winchester's 380-room castle and mansion at Basing on 14 October. Cromwell entered Devon on 24 October 1645 and remained there and in Cornwall until 12 April 1646. He met serious resistance only at Bovey Tracey (9 January), where he dispersed Thomas, Lord Wentworth's horse troop; Dartmouth (18 January), where he joined Fairfax in a carefully planned amphibious assault; and Torrington (16 February), where Ralph, Lord Hopton's force of 5000 men was dispersed. Otherwise it was an inexorable progress, occupying towns (the most important of which was Exeter) and castles from which the defenders had fled or were winkled out by delicate negotiation. After reporting briefly to parliament he returned to his command for the final seven-week siege of Oxford. Both Exeter and Oxford surrendered on extremely generous terms, with the royalists made liable only to minimal fines, lower than those set by parliamentary ordinance. It is worth noting Cromwell's strong support for these generous terms. He wanted to win the war as quickly as possible, not humiliate the losers.

The shoals of diplomacy, 1646–1647

3

The politics of peace

As this campaign progressed Cromwell's conviction that he was fighting God's cause became ever clearer to him. After the taking of Bletchingdon House in Oxfordshire in April 1645 he told his colleagues on the committee of both kingdoms that 'this was the mercy of God . . . God brought them to our hands when we looked not for them' (*Letters and Speeches*, 1904, letter 25, 9 April 1645). After Langport he was even more emphatic: 'thus you can see what the Lord hath wrought for us. Can any creature ascribe anything to itself? Now can we give all the glory to God!' But he added that when the 'mercy' of Langport be added to the 'mercy' of Naseby, then, 'is it not to see the face of God?' (ibid., 3.246–7, July 1645).

It was in this 'chain of providences' that Cromwell saw himself as the instrument of God's deeper purpose in bringing England through civil war: and Cromwell linked God's providential guidance more and more to the cause of religious liberty. Thus after Naseby Cromwell wrote to the Commons speaker and, following a staccato account of the battle, pleaded for religious liberty for all who served in a cause so obviously upheld by God: 'he that ventures his life for the liberty of his country, I wish he trust God for the liberty of his conscience, and you for the liberty he fights for' (ibid., letter 29, 14 June 1645). After the taking of Bristol in September he was plainer still: 'Presbyterians, Independents, all had the same spirit of faith and prayer ... they agree here, know no names of difference: pity it should be otherwise anywhere. All that believe have the same unity' (ibid., letter 31, 14 September 1645). The response of the Commons to these heartfelt pleas (as it was to be after the most passionate plea of all from the battlefield of Preston in 1648) was to censor the letters and to publish them with their pleas for liberty omitted, though in each case Lord Saye and other friends in the Lords procured the unlicensed printing of the whole letter some time later.

Cromwell returned to Westminster in July 1646 to face new challenges. As a soldier—and as an MP—he had spent four years committed to one overwhelming objective: to win the war. He had seen in councils of war and in parliamentary committees all too many of his colleagues reluctant to make the sacrifices necessary to secure victory. They were reluctant to tolerate the necessary requisitioning of supplies or the rough justice of war, reluctant to continue the fighting if there was a glimpse of a settlement by negotiation, reluctant to make use of men from less reputable social backgrounds or with fierce religious commitment. The rigidities of formal religion, the proscription on lay preaching, the inflexible Scottish demand for a strict, bureaucratic, and mandatory uniformity of belief and practice across the three kingdoms—all these things appalled him. While (as the artillery pounded out the prelude to a push of pike and a charge of horse) he meditated on how free prayer, free testimony, and the improvisation of worship had made God's immanence so clear, he must have been struck by the irrelevance and impropriety of the commitment to replacing one confessional state by another. But nothing in the molten politics of war prepared him for the low-temperature physics that were to constitute 'the politics of peace and the limits of the possible' (Davis, 141).

The twenty-two months between Cromwell's return to Westminster in July 1646 and the renewal of war in May 1648 saw him constantly on the move between London and wherever army headquarters were to be found. His commission as lieutenant-general formally lapsed in July 1646, but Fairfax paid no heed and spasmodically signed pay warrants for Cromwell in the months that followed. In May 1647 Cromwell submitted a statement of all his arrears to that point which was counter-signed and honoured. He attended some sessions of the army council as a parliamentary commissioner, but others (including Putney in October–November 1647) as 'lieutenant-general'. He was rewarded by parliament with estates in England and Ireland worth £2000 a year, and there were persistent rumours that as part of any settlement with the king made by the alliance of 'Independents' in parliament and their allies in the army, he would be created earl of Essex (the title held both by his own ancestor Thomas Cromwell and by the Bourchiers, and therefore assumed, erroneously, by many at the time to have been held by Elizabeth's ancestors). In the summer of 1646 his immediate family moved up from Ely to London to a town house in Drury Lane, where they remained until he was allocated rooms in the Cockpit, adjacent to the palace of Whitehall, after his return to London from the battle of Worcester in September 1651.

In the second half of 1646 Cromwell was one of the most active and dynamic members of parliament, serving on many central executive committees and acting as one of the most active tellers in the increasingly frequent divisions. But little is recoverable of his contribution to debates, although he can be seen to have remained close to those who had constituted the war party throughout the civil wars: Henry Vane, Oliver St John, Nathaniel Fiennes in the Commons, William Fiennes, Viscount Saye and Sele, and Philip, Lord Wharton, in the Lords. He seems to have been constantly in the Palace of Westminster until overwhelmed with a life-threatening (but unidentified) illness that kept him house-bound throughout February 1647 and on half-throttle for some weeks thereafter. Few of his letters from the second half of 1646 and the first half of 1647 have survived, though those that have reveal continued support for godly, honest folk persecuted because they would not attend their parish churches.

King, parliament, and army

By the time Cromwell was back in the political saddle in March 1647 a crisis had erupted in the relations between parliament and the army. A majority in both houses was determined to bring about a settlement of the three kingdoms. The Scots would be paid off and sent home; most of the New Model would be disbanded and the rest restructured and dispatched to put an end to the Irish rebellion; and intense negotiations with the king would settle the remaining issues. Those negotiations would seek to honour the solemn commitment to replace the Elizabethan church settlement with a presbyterian settlement enshrined in the proposals that had been hammered out in the Anglo–Scottish Westminster assembly. The king would lose the freedom to choose his own ministers and the right to control the armed forces; and the proponents of this settlement would promote themselves to high political and court offices. There was much here for Cromwell and his parliamentary allies, and even more for the army, to resent. But when the army petitioned against the proposals, the Commons declared their very act of petitioning unlawful. This inaugurated a six-month-long crisis, during which Cromwell's role was consistent: to prevent a formal rupture; to persuade the houses that the anger in the army was considerable and reasonable; and to persuade the army that men like himself could bring parliament to listen to their grievances. The rumours picked up and reported by the French ambassador that Cromwell was considering abandoning England in the spring for a senior command under the elector palatine amid the dying embers of the Thirty Years' War were almost certainly false. Cromwell was working to prevent the parliamentarian movement from disintegrating.

Thus from 2 to 20 May 1647 Cromwell was one of the four officers/MPs sent down from parliament to army headquarters in Saffron Walden to discuss how the army's grievances about arrears, indemnity, and war pensions could be addressed. On 21 May he and Charles Fleetwood reported back to the Commons on the state of the army. The document he carried bore the legend 'the heads of a report ... in the name of themselves and the rest of the officers in the army and the members of that House lately sent down' (*Clarke Papers*, 1.94–9). Like a classic negotiator he understated to each party the disaffection of the other towards it. And the result, late in May, was disaster. Having assured the houses that the army would disband quietly if its legitimate concerns about arrears and indemnity were addressed, Cromwell watched in horror as the Commons voted the immediate disbandment of most of the army on the basis of meagre concessions. Perhaps the Commons thought that since the Scots had sulkily returned home and disbanded on the basis of a small down-payment and vague promises for the future, so would the New Model. It was not to be.

From the time he returned to London, Cromwell's house in Drury Lane was constantly visited by a stream of sectaries and officers. There they were 'frugally entertained by Mrs Cromwell with small beer, bread and butter [as] they laid bare to the lieutenant general their fear of the presbyterians and their ideas for the army's salvation' (Gentles, 169). There was nothing unique, therefore, in a visit by a cornet in Fairfax's regiment of horse, George Joyce, on 31 May. What he and Cromwell discussed is not known for sure. Most likely it was a request that the 'presbyterian' officers guarding the king at Holdenby House in Northampton be replaced by more reliable officers, who were less likely to be at the beck and call of the 'presbyterian' politicians at Westminster. It is likely that Joyce informed Cromwell that

he had gathered 1000 horse (almost two full regiments) and that he sought Cromwell's informal authorization for him to surprise Colonel Graves and his 100 men at Holdenby and remove the distrusted officers. But to commission—however informally—a cornet to humiliate a colonel seems incredible.

Perhaps Cromwell was not told the whole story; or perhaps he was asked to put himself or someone of appropriate rank in charge of the expedition and declined to do so, only for Joyce to undertake it anyway. What is almost certain is that Joyce originally intended to keep the king at Holdenby under his own authority, but that after the escape of Graves he panicked and started moving Charles across the country to army headquarters at Newmarket. As the news broke, Fairfax sent Colonel Edward Whalley to intercept Joyce and the king and to return the latter to Holdenby. But Whalley acceded to the king's stated preference to be taken to Newmarket. Cromwell and the other generals both at the time and later solemnly protested to both king and parliament that Joyce had acted 'without their privity, knowledge or consent' (Warwick, 229). Joyce later maintained otherwise and there were plenty at the time and later who were unconvinced by Cromwell's denials. It was the first of a whole series of occasions (the king's escape from Hampton Court to the Isle of Wight, Pride's Purge, the dissolution of the Rump, the self-immolation of the nominated assembly, the offer of the crown in February 1657) when Cromwell solemnly denied something which other principals and other contemporary witnesses asserted—that he was guilty of underhand dealing to secure his goals.

And as with all the others, conclusive proof either way is lacking.

The seizure of the king escalated the crisis at Westminster. Cromwell now stayed with the army and took a leading part in the debates among the general officers and in the general council of the army: generals, regimental commanders, and representatives (or adjutators) of the junior officers and of the rank and file who met at least fortnightly over the following months. With ever greater determination the general council clarified the terms of the future settlement of the kingdom and their right to articulate those terms. On 7 June 1647, at Childerley House near Cambridge, Cromwell had his first interview with King Charles. He was to have several more during August and September. From mid-July, with the explicit consent of the general council, Commissary-General Henry Ireton (Oliver's close colleague in the defence of the Isle of Ely, and since 15 June 1646 his son-in-law), together with Cromwell and other senior commanders, and in close liaison with their friends in the two houses, drafted *The Heads of Proposals*. These were to be simultaneously proffered to the king and converted into a series of parliamentary bills to be passed by the houses and then formally assented to and made binding by the royal assent.

This orderly stratagem was shaken by the violent mass demonstrations in favour of peace and disbandment in London on 26 July 1647 that caused sixty-five MPs to withdraw from London to the protection of the army. This led to the army's occupation of London, its reinstatement of the sixty-five, and its removal of the eleven leading

presbyterians whom the army called 'incendiaries'. Cromwell probably resumed his seat in the wake of this *putsch* but he spent more time at army headquarters at Putney than in the house until late September. Thus in August he was central to the failed head-to-head negotiations with a king who would never say yes and never say no. In September and October a different tack was tried. The houses—the presbyterians now cowed and in a minority—worked steadily on the bills that would enact the proposals. Cromwell was then pivotal to pushing several of those bills, especially a toleration bill, which repealed the Elizabethan statutes requiring church attendance and permitted anyone who wished 'to hear the word of God preached elsewhere'. He still expected to be able to bounce both king and parliament into a settlement.

The Heads of Proposals would have exempted very few 'malignant' royalists from pardon, they would have placed time-limited restrictions on Charles's freedom to choose his own ministers or control the armed forces, and they would have restored the episcopalian church as the Church of England but without the right to require either attendance or obedience to its forms or beliefs. Under these proposals parliaments would have been elected regularly on a rationalized franchise but would not have been omnicompetent or omnipresent. They would have met for a limited period every two years. Much of *The Heads of Proposals* foreshadowed the 'Instrument of government' under which Cromwell became lord protector in December 1653. Until mid-October, Cromwell and his allies seemed to be holding the ring. But then, in quick succession, he was to find himself defied by parliament, by large sections of the army, and by the king.

The Putney debates

The post-war settlement to which Cromwell was now firmly committed assumed a divided sovereignty between king and parliament. There were many who felt that this was no longer sufficient. Foremost among these were the London pamphleteers shortly to become known as the Levellers. These men argued with ever greater force for a literal 'agreement of the people', whereby all householders would sign up to put themselves under a new form of government in which all those who exercised authority—above all the chief and lesser magistrates, and members of parliament—were accountable to those who elected them. The king would not be party to the making of the agreement but would be offered a limited role within it on a take-it-or-leave-it basis. Most of the adjutators had worked closely with the generals and had consented to their face-to-face negotiations with the king. But some of them now began to doubt the probity of Cromwell and Ireton—perhaps influenced by the growing disaffection towards the 'grandees' in the army and the parliament expressed in the writings of the Leveller leader John Lilburne, beginning with the characterization of Cromwell and Vane as 'the sons of Machiavel' (J. Lilburne, *Jonah's Cry out of the Whale's Belly*, July 1647, 3). From about 29 September some regiments began to choose additional 'agents' who would make that case more forcefully. The result was a tense series of debates in and around Putney church from 28 October to 11 November 1647. The debates were covered by a news blackout so complete that there is no contemporary discussion of them. The secretary to the council of the army, William Clarke, used a team of stenographers to cover the opening days of the debate, but from 2 November tensions rose so high that even this recording was discontinued. His minutes were never published and were unknown until rediscovered in 1890 by Sir Charles Firth.

Cromwell's role at Putney was first and foremost to be chairman and ringmaster. His mission statement for all four recorded days was 'let us be doing, but let us be united in our doing' (*Clarke Papers*, 1.259). He extracted a retraction of the charge that he and his son-in-law had negotiated in bad faith. The *Agreement of the People*, tabled on 28 October, proposed that the discredited king and the discredited parliament be ignored and a new constitution introduced in a new social compact signed by all those who wished to enjoy rights of citizenship. Cromwell subsequently persuaded a committee of eighteen, made up of grandees, officer adjutators, and soldier adjutators to whom the most contentious issues were referred, unanimously to reject that proposition in favour of a proposal that the army lobby the Long Parliament to dissolve itself after making provision for a redistribution of seats 'according to some rule of equality of proportion' (ibid., 1.365), and for biennial elections on a franchise consisting of all those previously qualified plus all those who had secured a stake by offering their lives in the parliamentarian armies up to and including the date of the battle of Naseby. This compromise, acceptable to all sections of the army, was made possible by Cromwell's careful diplomacy.

Up to the evening of 31 October tempers were frayed but things were going reasonably well. Unity had been maintained. But Cromwell had more difficulty in controlling things on and after 1 November. Now the subject turned to the right of the king and the Lords to veto legislation approved by the Commons. This drifted into the wider and even more contentious issue of whether the king should be a party to the settlement and even whether Charles should be deposed (by implication even executed). Adjutator Edward Sexby proclaimed that 'we have gone about to heal Babylon when she would not' (*Clarke Papers*, 1.377); Cromwell responded by saying that there were many problems with Charles—'we all apprehend danger from the person of the king'—and that there could be no safety in such a person 'having the least interest in the public affairs of the kingdom', but they should not jump to the conclusion that 'God will destroy these persons' (kings in general) or 'that power' (monarchy). He did not rule out deposition, but he did not see any immediate divine encouragement to proceed with it (ibid., 1.378–82).

Clearly by November 1647 Cromwell's patience with Charles was running out. But he also argued that the army should not be 'wedded and glued to forms of government' and that 'forms of government are (as St Paul says) dross and dung in comparison of Christ' (*Clarke Papers*, 1.277, 370). Using the Old Testament as his sole source he argued that the Jewish people had done well and badly under all forms of government. A bad king did not discredit monarchy itself. Cromwell's speeches on 1 November 1647 testify to the development of an unsophisticated political thought which owed nothing to Aristotle or Edward Coke and everything to the Old Testament. They are also testimony to his growing impatience with Charles and his willingness to wait upon God's pronouncement of a judgment against the king. The debates on 1 November spiralled out of control and somebody may have told William Clarke to stop recording them. Debate continued for another ten days, during which Ireton stormed out but Cromwell stayed. The debates seem to have centred on the role of the king in the making of the settlement and increasingly on whether he should be deposed. In a fascinating fragment left in his papers for 11 November, Clarke records that Colonel Harrison called Charles 'a man of blood', and that 'they were to prosecute him'. Cromwell replied by 'putting several cases in which murder was not to be punished', citing the case of King David's refusal to put his nephew Joab on trial for killing Abner, because his other nephews, as military governors with more force at their disposal than David himself had, would rise up to prevent or to avenge Joab's death: 'the sons of Zeruiah were too hard for him' (ibid., 1.417). Charles I, Cromwell implies, no longer deserved to reign; but it was not feasible or prudent at present to get rid of him.

The Putney debates broke up acrimoniously. But in the ensuing recriminations the fault-line lay not between those who wanted a cautious extension of the franchise and a radical one but—a very different alignment—between those who wanted to break off all personal negotiations with the king and those who did not. Fairfax and Cromwell struggled to maintain army unity, and they strove to do so by holding a series of separate army rendezvous. They succeeded, but only at the expense of a tense confrontation with mutineers who appeared against orders at the first rendezvous at Ware.

Cromwell, riding among sullen ranks of troopers, pulled copies of the *Agreement of the People* from their hatbands and ordered them back to their quarters. The mutiny did not spread from the initial two (of twenty-four) regiments. By 18 November order was restored.

Putney seems to have been a turning point for Cromwell. He came to realize that his brokering a settlement with Charles was not acceptable to large sections of the army, and he may well have recognized that the king had not been negotiating in good faith. On 12 November his growing distrust was massively reinforced. Charles, breaking his word, escaped from Hampton Court and fled to the Isle of Wight. There was plenty of contemporary speculation that Cromwell encouraged him in this escapade, but there are compelling reasons for doubting it. When a few days later Sir John Berkeley, a royalist intermediary who had formed good relations with Cromwell and Ireton over recent months, arrived with a letter from Charles, he found an army council meeting in progress. He later recalled that 'I look'd upon Cromwell and Ireton and the rest of my acquaintance, who saluted me very coldly, and had their countenance quite changed towards me'. Berkeley was then told by an unnamed officer that at the afternoon meeting of the council Ireton and Cromwell had called for the king to be transferred as a close prisoner to London where the army would then 'bring him to a tryal'; and that 'none be allowed to speak to' (negotiate with) the king, 'upon pain of death' (*The Memoirs of Sir John Berkeley*, 1699, 70, 72).

War and regicide, 1648–1649

4

The second civil war

Between 11 November 1647 and 3 May 1648 Cromwell can be glimpsed sometimes in London, sometimes at army headquarters. There are extant only fragmentary parliamentary diaries from this time, but one of them offers a single glimpse of Cromwell's unfolding views. Speaking in the Commons on 3 January 1648 (according to a much-repeated royalist canard rattling his sword in its scabbard as he spoke) he passionately demanded a suspension of all 'addresses' to the king for the foreseeable future. He asserted that they 'shalt not suffer a hypocrite to reign' and that they 'should not any longer expect safety and government from an obstinate man whose heart God had hardened'. Even more dramatically, he said that 'we declared our intentions for monarchy ... unless necessity enforce an alteration' (D. Underdown, 'Parliamentary diary of John Boys, 1647–8', *Bulletin of the Institute of Historical Research*, 39, 1966, 156). (Necessity for Cromwell meant seeking out and obeying God's will in his providences: the authority to settle the kingdom, he told his nominated assembly in 1653, came to them 'by way of Necessity, by the way of the wise Providence of God' (*Speeches*, 20, 4 July 1653).) Later the same day Cromwell wrote to his cousin by marriage Colonel Robert Hammond, custodian of Charles in Carisbrooke Castle, that the king's flight and subsequent developments represented 'a mighty providence to this poor kingdom and to us all'. This gives a rather chilling menace to his concluding words: 'we shall (I hope) instantly go upon the business in relation to [the king], tending to prevent danger' and his request that Hammond 'search out' any 'juggling' by the king (*Letters and Speeches*, 1904, letter 52, 3 January 1648).

Cromwell's realization at Putney that the king did not deserve restoration but that the army must await a sign from God about when and how to proceed against him was powerfully reinforced by the king's escape. During 1648 there are indications that Cromwell was considering how the king might be induced to abdicate in favour of one of his sons. The generally well-informed Roman agent in London, writing on 17 January, names Cromwell and Oliver St John as favouring direct negotiation with the prince of Wales which could have led to Charles's abdication or deposition. The French ambassador and material in the papers of the duke of Hamilton support the suggestion that there was such a plan, although they do not name the men behind it. Later in the year ambassadorial sources indicate that Cromwell was looking to replace Charles by the king's youngest son, Henry, duke of Gloucester.

For much of the spring, as a series of regional revolts rocked the parliamentarian regime, and as the Scots prepared for an invasion to restore the king on the rather vague terms he had agreed in a secret treaty signed on 26 December 1647, Cromwell's whereabouts are not generally known. He was, however, present for some but not all of the three-day prayer meeting at Windsor held from 29 April to 1 May 1648. It ended with the council of officers binding themselves to call 'Charles Stuart, that man of bloud, to an account, for that bloud he had shed, and mischief he had done, to his utmost, against the Lords cause and people in these poor Nations' (W. Allen, *A Faithful Memorial*, 1659, 5).

On 3 May Fairfax divided the New Model Army, keeping the larger part in the south-east to deal with the bush fires of rebellion in Kent and East Anglia and sending Cromwell with five regiments to deal with revolts in south Wales. Cromwell quickly took Chepstow and Tenby, but without heavy artillery he found no way to storm the great castle of Pembroke. It took him six weeks to starve it into surrender. By then the Scots were marching on England and he had hastily to march north. He joined up with northern regiments under the command of John Lambert at Knaresborough, and together they crossed the Pennines and fell upon the Scots as they advanced through Lancashire. Preston was his first battle in full command. It was a messy three-day affair (17–19 August 1648) in which he secured a complete victory, aided by very poor communication among the Scottish commanders and by torrential rain that soaked the powder of the Scottish infantry and rendered it useless. But the outcome owed most of all to Cromwell's decisive and bold leadership. By the end of 19 August the army of the Scottish engagers had been annihilated: Cromwell reckoned 2000 killed and 9000 taken prisoner. He promptly set off and made straight for Edinburgh. There he found that the marquess of Argyll—who had always opposed the English adventure—had seized power. Leaving Lambert and three regiments (at Argyll's request) to shore up this regime, Cromwell moved south and quickly reduced Carlisle and Berwick, but became bogged down in stamping out the embers of revolt in Yorkshire.

The death of the king

As Cromwell campaigned in 1648 there was a dramatic development in his religious thinking. His letter to his cousin Elizabeth St John in 1638 describing his religious conversion had been saturated in biblical images, but his letters throughout the 1640s used the Bible only as glancing asides. Suddenly in 1648 his letters become meditations on how particular scriptures were helping him to find his way through the constitutional mire. Private letters to Fairfax, to Philip Wharton, Lord Wharton, to Robert Hammond, and to Oliver St John were epistolary sermons exploring the will of God. After parliament had voted to reopen negotiations with the king Cromwell, from the siege of Pembroke, wrote to Fairfax and told him that 'surely it is not [the mind of God] that the poor people of this kingdom should still be made the object of wrath and anger, nor that our God would have our necks under a yoke of bondage'. And he continued:

> for these things that have lately come to pass have been the wonderful works of God, breaking the rod of the oppressor as in the day of Midian, not with garments much rolled in blood but by the terror of the Lord; who will yet save His people and confound His enemies as in that day. (*Letters and Speeches*, 1904, letter 61, 28 June 1648)

This is a paraphrase of Isaiah chapter 9 and contains a cross-reference to the victory of Gideon and the Midianites described in the book of Judges. Gideon was the farmer called from the plough to winnow and lead the armies of Israel. He defeated the Midianites, executed their kings, and then returned to his farm. It is one of several references to the Gideon story in Cromwell's letters in 1648—suggesting that he saw himself as the new Gideon. After the battle of Preston meditations on Psalms 17 and 105 led him to tell parliament that 'they that are implacable and will not leave troubling the land may be speedily destroyed out of the land' (ibid., letter 64, 20 August 1648).

Who else could he mean but the king? Once again the Commons published his letter with the lecture at the end omitted. In a private letter a week later to Wharton he called down God's mercy on 'the whole society of saints, despised, jeered saints' (ibid., letter 68, 2 September 1648) and on the same day told Oliver St John that 'this scripture hath been great stay with me: read it; Isaiah eighth [chapter], [verses] 10, 11, 14, read all the chapter' (ibid., letter 67, 2 September 1648). Isaiah predicted Ahaz's turning from God would condemn his kingdom to inevitable collapse, but that a godly remnant would survive the holocaust. Cromwell was using the scriptures to discern God's will, and he was ever more convinced that one way or another Charles I had to be removed from the land.

As he mopped up royalist resistance in the north Cromwell was at least spasmodically aware of the fast-moving events in the south, above all of the content of the *Remonstrance* of the army (20 November 1648). This was both an unwavering repudiation of the parliament's decision to reopen negotiations with a king who would dishonour any treaty he made, and a demand that 'the capital and grand author of our troubles, the person of the king...may be speedily brought to justice for the treason, blood and mischief he is guilty of' (pp. 62–5). It also demanded that the king's elder sons, the prince of Wales and the duke of York, surrender themselves for trial on pain of being declared incapable of governing and sentenced to die if found in England. The phrase 'person of the king' and the careful wording of the section on the princes Charles and James suggest that Ireton and his colleagues may have envisaged not the end of monarchy but the replacement of Charles by Prince Henry, duke of Gloucester, who was in their custody. Cromwell's letters showed that he supported the *Remonstrance.* Two letters written to Hammond in November pleaded with him to take his orders from his military and not his parliamentary masters and study the 'so constant, so clear and unclouded' providences of God. He called the Newport treaty on which the houses were embarked 'this ruining, hypocritical agreement' and begged Hammond to consider what good could come from a treaty with the king, 'this man against whom the Lord hath witnessed' (*Letters and Speeches*, 1904, letter 85, 25 November 1648; ibid., 3.389–92, 6 November 1648) .

There is no further reliable evidence of Cromwell's intentions until after he had returned to Westminster, upon a peremptory order from Fairfax, late on 6 December, hours after Pride's Purge during which some MPs were arrested and many more turned away following the Commons' defiant vote to continue negotiating with the king. He took his seat in the Commons the next morning and immediately tried to calm things down and to prevent any hasty action. Foreign ambassadors clearly thought he hoped to induce the king to abdicate, and his role in sending the earl of Denbigh (who had been involved in earlier attempts to get Charles to abdicate in favour of the prince of Wales) to negotiate with the king on an unknown brief points that way. Bulstrode Whitelocke, whose evidence was committed to paper shortly afterwards, appears to confirm that the mission was intended to offer the king his life in return for an abdication.

It was not that Cromwell had any constitutional scruple about a trial and deposition, even about execution; rather, he had the overwhelming sense that such action would be counter-productive, that there would be an internal and international reaction so violent as to sweep away those who had engineered it. The sons of Zeruiah would be too strong for them. Presbyterians thundered from their pulpits. The king of France, the Dutch estates (who had just made a naval treaty with the king's lord lieutenant in Ireland), and the Scottish estates all threatened and cajoled the army leaders and the Rumpers to spare the king. Cromwell sought desperately to broaden the support for the 6 December coup and to delay a trial. As the king refused to contemplate abdication, a trial became inevitable, a trial during which negotiation under duress could continue. For six weeks Cromwell worked for a settlement without a regicide, but once he concluded that Charles would not abdicate, not only the king's trial but his death became inevitable. To try to put someone else on the throne so long as the king lived was even worse than to attempt, in the face of the inevitable backlash across the British Isles and western Europe, to establish a kingless

Commonwealth. And so, in the final ten days of January, he worked for the latter. He attended every day of the trial and was the third to append his name to the death warrant. Legends attached themselves to Cromwell's actions, but none is reliable. Algernon Sidney later claimed that Cromwell told him the army would cut off the king's head with the crown upon it. Colonel Isaac Ewer claimed that Cromwell and Henry Marten flicked ink at one another in a childish game after signing the warrant. Clarendon claimed that Cromwell and others compelled Richard Ingoldsby and others to sign, holding their hands to the parchment. The only credible story of this kind is the testimony of Philip Warwick that as Cromwell looked down on the dismembered royal corpse, he murmured: 'Cruel necessity'. God's providences were not always comfortable.

Cromwell in January 1649

Cromwell was now the single most powerful man in England. Fairfax was still the lord general and Cromwell his lieutenant-general. But the events of the previous three months had knocked the stuffing out of Fairfax. He had hoped against hope that the king would see sense but when the crunch came and he had to decide whether to assert his authority as head of the army to attempt to halt the trial, or more particularly the regicide, he had alternately wrung his hands and sat on them. Before him stretched a decade of irresolution. He did not resign his command for another sixteen months, but Cromwell was *de facto* general from the moment the king's head was cut off on 30 January 1649. In parliament, Cromwell was prominent but not dominant.

In the public eye this position was also consolidated. Cromwell's image was one of the best known by 1649, appearing in many pamphlets and broadsheets. For example, as early as 1644 he was pictured among the successful generals in *The Parliament's Kalendar of Black Saints*, and he makes a prominent appearance in John Vicars's *England's Worthies* (1647). His name was much more familiar than his image. Between his first appearance in the early summer of 1643 and the end of 1648, Cromwell's name had appeared on the title-pages of 119 pamphlets, 79 of them in the year 1648. This was low visibility in comparison with the attention given to Fairfax (named on 654 title-pages before the end of 1648) but it was high compared with others who were still alive. In total about 90 per cent of commentators gave a broadly sympathetic account of his military career (just as every engraved image of Cromwell portrays him in the armour of a cavalry commander). Press coverage of his disagreements with army colleagues was short-lived in 1643–5, but from June 1647 he became the target of sustained personal abuse. It began with Lilburne, who singled out Cromwell, together with Henry Ireton, for criticism in a string of polemical pamphlets beginning with *Jonah's Cry out of the Whale's Belly* (July), and *The Juglers Discovered* (late September). But simultaneously there came criticism from royalist and (renewed) criticism from presbyterian sources, and a personal crusade mounted by William Prynne (*The Hypocrite Unmasked* and *Articles of the Impeachment for High Treason*). And there was a flurry of short, witty satires (*A Coppie of a Letter* by John Worth-rush, *Cromwell's Panegyrick*, *Craftie Cromwell*, *The Machiavellian Cromwellist*, and *A Case for Nol Cromwell's Nose*). The charges brought from all sides were the same:

vaunting ambition, machiavellianism, hypocrisy, insincerity. He was accused specifically of using a personal treaty with the king to line his own pocket and secure the earldom of Essex, the title having lapsed with the death of the third earl. He was also accused of manipulating Fairfax—'Sir Thomas Fairfax was but a cypher with you, Cromwell, only your conductor' (*The Hypocrite Unmasked*, 2).

Rather surprisingly, in the years immediately after the regicide Cromwell's name receded from public view, appearing on title-pages forty-one times in 1649 (entirely related to his campaigns in Ireland), twenty-nine times in 1650, nineteen times in 1651, and fourteen times in 1652. Once again it was his military conduct and achievements that dominated and apart from Leveller and royalist protests about his role in the early months of 1649 most of the coverage was positive or at least neutral and descriptive.

Cromwell did not commit to paper his ideas for the settlement of the kingdom in the wake of the regicide. He had come to see the need to eliminate Charles I but there is no evidence that he believed in the permanent eradication of monarchy. It might not be feasible immediately, but nothing about the Rump Parliament was a blueprint for the future. When he helped to draw up *The Heads of Proposals* in July 1647 he was clearly committed to the constitutional and religious settlement there provided for, and all that changed between July 1647 and January 1649 was an unwillingness to have Charles I as the man to serve as constitutional monarch within that framework. He was thus a soldier whose pragmatism had driven him to king-killing. He had become a hesitant politician, all too aware of the huge risks associated with regicide: the extreme difficulty of creating any stability on the basis of an act bound to cause widespread revulsion and a tidal wave of international protest. His instincts were to do everything possible to broaden the basis of support for the embattled regime, opening the doors to anyone willing to walk through them.

Cromwell's social thought was no more impetuous. In 1643 he had shown a willingness to promote men for the vigour and strength of their commitment to the cause of liberty without regard to their social status. But he had not shown that hostility towards the peerage and gentry of which he was accused by Manchester and Crawford. On the contrary, throughout the period from 1644 to 1648 he worked closely with individual peers, especially Saye and Wharton, and many of his close allies in the Commons, including Nathaniel Fiennes and Oliver St John, were related to peers. On 1 November 1647, as Ireton struggled to hold the line at Putney against the calls for manhood suffrage by arguing for a franchise based on the possession of a 'fixed permanent interest', Cromwell sat mute. More than forty speeches were delivered that day before he joined in, and the argument had by then progressed beyond the argument for social prudence.

Cromwell's religious views are better chronicled but not straightforward. He was always in favour of a national church to which the great majority should be attached. He believed in a publicly approved and appointed ministry supported by some form of mandatory levy on all householders—tithes until a better system could be worked out. He believed that all sincere protestants who wished to dissociate themselves from that national church and worship

God in the light of their own consciences should be permitted to do so. He came over time to define more precisely but not necessarily more strictly how to prevent the liberty he strove to promote from being (in his own eyes) abused. He was suspicious of all clerical claims to special or reserved powers, and believed that gifted laymen should be allowed to preach and lay people to prophesy. He believed that membership of the national church should not privilege anyone in the distribution of offices and responsibilities in civil and military affairs. He expected all those who claimed liberty for themselves to be willing to grant it to others. Beyond that, little is clear.

There is nothing to indicate how Cromwell himself worshipped. He was married in a London parish church in 1620, almost certainly in accordance with the Book of Common Prayer. The registration of all his children in parish registers in the 1620s and 1630s suggests a continued willingness to participate at some level in the life of the church. But he seems also to have played a leading part in a house-conventicle and to have preached at it. It is not known whether he continued to exercise the gift of preaching as an army officer. It cannot be shown that he ever in his life received holy communion. It is likely but not certain that he sometimes attended divine worship in a parish church after 1640, and he probably worshipped in the old Chapel Royal at Whitehall in the 1650s and heard sermons there. Most of the ministers who were his chaplains were Independents, but of the kind who were willing to hold livings in the state church as reconstituted in and after 1650. One of his sisters, who married John Wilkins, the warden of Wadham College, Oxford (and after the Restoration bishop of Chester), almost certainly married in his presence in the Chapel Royal in 1656 using the marriage service from the Book of Common Prayer. Within a period of four weeks in 1647 he appears openly to have supported the restoration of an episcopate shorn of all coercive power, the introduction of what Robert Baillie called 'a lame erastian presbytery' for an experimental period, and the right of laymen to preach and to administer the sacraments.

Cromwell, then, was no more wedded to forms of government in the church than in the state. They too were dross and dung in comparison with the authentic search for Christian living, and God would not be confined in his choice of instruments. In the 1640s Cromwell struggled within the puritan movement to liberate those who could not in good conscience abide the rules being made by the godly men in power. In the 1650s he had to decide what to do with those who abused the liberty he strove to nurture: what to do about the licentious, the blasphemous, and the idolatrous. Although this may have made him seem more restrictive in his religious views, it is not clear that this was not a mirage created by the responsibilities of power.

Ordering three kingdoms, 1649–1651

5

Dealing with the Rump Parliament

Over the next four years Cromwell combined the demanding business of war with the demanding business of sustaining a fragile political system and of seeking to develop viable long-term political and institutional forms. He was away from London, campaigning in Ireland and in Scotland, from July 1649 to mid-September 1651. But he kept in close touch with events there during his absences, and after 12 September 1651 he never left the environs of the capital (except for two brief excursions into Kent in May 1652) for the rest of his life, moving first to the Cockpit and then, early in 1654, into the royal palaces at Whitehall and Hampton Court.

Cromwell's role in the Rump Parliament was an uncomfortable one. For some he was God's chosen instrument, the man manifestly enjoying the Lord's favour and therefore one who could deliver the fruits of revolution. To others he was the man who had the ultimate say in what happened because he had the army behind him, and the army had shown in July 1647 and in December 1648 that its patience could snap and that it would have its way. And so everyone looked to him for a lead and he found himself pulled in different directions. The central tension in him which cruelly tugged at him in the internal forum was that 'between on the one hand his taste for constitutional respectability and on the other his hunger for godly reformation' (Worden, *Rump Parliament*, 274). This was vividly expressed in the external circumstances that he brought about: after

> the trial and execution of the king, he helped to ensure that the settlement which followed was as respectable as possible, and that power would remain in the hands of unrevolutionary men. Enthusiasm for godly reformation was not the criterion he adopted when he sought to determine the character and composition of the Rump government. When he later demanded such reformation of the Rump, it not surprisingly declined to grant it. (ibid., 19)

From the moment he returned to London on 6 December 1648 Cromwell was desperate to broaden the basis of support for the new regime. Before the regicide little could be accomplished, although he worked to secure the early release of those imprisoned. But from 1 February 1649 onwards he actively encouraged those who had been excluded in December, or who had excluded themselves in protest, to return. He targeted especially the 'Royal Independents', those like Lord Saye and his son Nathaniel Fiennes with whom he had worked closely in 1647 and who had wanted a settlement with the king along the lines of *The Heads of Proposals*. Even though only one of them, Oliver St John, was persuaded to take his seat, Cromwell continued to work on the others and keep their seats warm for them.

His aim was to tell them that what was done was done, and that sulking would not bring the king back. Therefore they should face the reality that the king was dead and work for the programme of social, legal, and religious reform to which they had so long been committed. Even more dramatic was his doomed attempt to save the House of Lords from abolition, and his successful subversion of Ireton's attempt to make all those who served on the Rump's executive, the council of state, take an oath that recognized the legitimacy of the purge and the regicide. As a result twenty-two of its forty-one members failed to give any assent to the actions that had brought into being the regime they headed. Cromwell was, of course, himself on the council—indeed its president in its first weeks until 8 March 1649—though his closest military colleagues at this time, Henry Ireton and Thomas Harrison, were pointedly excluded.

Cromwell's aim was simple: to prevent the regime from collapsing and all the forces of vengeance and reaction from overwhelming the new Commonwealth. The spectre of foreign intervention, the prospect of royalist invasion from Ireland and Scotland, and the need to get men of goodwill up and down the land to collect the taxes and mobilize the supplies that would allow the regime to protect itself, all demanded an embrace of the offended. This in turn led him to abandon the commitment of the previous eighteen months to an orderly transfer of power to a new parliament elected by a reformed franchise. This had to await the stabilization of the regime. Thus the second *Agreement of the People*, hammered out by Ireton and other army officers, by radicals in parliament and the City of London, and by the Levellers in the weeks either side of the Purge, and with much, perhaps all, of which Cromwell was in sympathy, had also to be shelved for the time being. When the Levellers inevitably took this as the ultimate proof of Cromwell's (and Ireton's) duplicity they subjected the generals to a blistering series of attacks, most notably in *England's New Chains Discovered* and *The Hunting of the Foxes by the Five Small Beagles*. They launched their own third *Agreement of the People* and looked to their friends in the army to mutiny against their traitorous generals, linking the failure to promote the second agreement to the understandable reluctance of many soldiers to go on the impending expedition to Ireland. Fairfax and Cromwell were compelled to march with 4000 men to the Cotswolds in a short, fierce campaign in late April and early May to put down these mutinies at Burford.

Thus Cromwell in 1649 stood full-square behind the cruel necessity of executing Charles I and the current necessity of governing through the remnant of the Long Parliament who had accepted the purge or who had been willing to contaminate themselves by re-entry after the regicide. He neither approved nor disapproved of the Rump at this stage: it was an interim expedient that was keeping open the prospect of a new freedom from royal and clerical tyranny.

Over the next two years Cromwell was away on campaign. He did not try to exercise much influence over what happened in the Rump or the council of state (declining to become involved, for example, in the debate about whether to go to war with the Dutch), but he was much lobbied by all groups. Far more of his incoming correspondence than of his outgoing letters has survived, and it is clear that he was courted by all those groups who were conforming to the new regime. He in turn continued to write to old friends who had washed their hands of the revolution. Thus he wrote a striking letter to Lord Wharton from winter quarters in Ireland, likening his chastening work there to the action of Phinehas who thrust his spear through an Israelite and a Midianite concubine as they were copulating and thus brought to an end the plague that was a sign of God's wrath. He also defended what the Rump was achieving despite itself: 'good kept out; most bad remaining. It hath been so these nine years, yet God has wrought. The greatest work lasts; and is still at work' (*Letters and Speeches*, 1904, letter 117, 1 January 1650).

Cromwell in Ireland

Cromwell had no known connection with Irish affairs before the outbreak of the Irish rising in November 1641. He can then be seen making a generous gift (£300 on 1 February 1642) and a significant loan against confiscated Irish land (£500—more than his annual income is supposed to have been—in April 1642). In the months before the outbreak of civil war in England he was one of the most active members of the committee for the affairs of Ireland and two other committees charged with funding the Anglo-Scottish military expedition. For example, he attended thirty-three of the thirty-nine meetings of the main committee in the months from April to July 1642. When he was in London during the years 1643–6 he played little part in Irish affairs and he was not appointed to committees for Irish affairs. There is evidence that he wished to be appointed to command the new military expedition to Ireland in 1647, but that post went to

Philip Skippon. In 1648 he handed over two-thirds of the £1680 per annum income awarded him out of the earl of Worcester's estates for the Irish war. When Fairfax declined to command the expedition to overthrow the loyalist alliance of the marquess of Ormond and the Catholic confederates in 1649, the position fell to Cromwell as much because of his seniority as because of his developed interest in Ireland.

Cromwell was appointed in May 1649 to be lord lieutenant of Ireland and to be general of the army there, although technically as part of the New Model Army still under Fairfax's nominal command. He had three principal objectives in crossing to Ireland. The first was to eliminate the threat of military support for Charles II from those loyal to him—principally the Old English (protestant and Catholic) supporters of the long-time loyalist lord lieutenant James Butler, marquess of Ormond, and the Old English and Irish Catholic supporters of the confederation of Kilkenny. The second was to carry through the confiscation of land from all those involved in rebellion against the English parliament since 1641 and the redistribution of confiscated land to those who had invested (as 'adventurers') in various military expeditions since 1642. The third was to reform the institutions of Ireland not only (or specifically) to introduce the instruments of English civility, but to improve on them. This commitment can most clearly be seen in his proposals for law reform. On 31 December 1649 Cromwell wrote to invite John Sadler, a Cambridge don and civil lawyer, to become chief justice of Munster to establish 'a way of doing justice amongst these poor people which, for the uprightness and cheapness of it, may exceedingly gain upon them' (*Letters and Speeches*, 1904, 3.267, 31 December 1649). Sadler turned him down but his offer was accepted by John Cook, prosecutor of the king at his trial. Cook set to work to provide swift and cheap justice, dispensing with most court officials, radically reducing fees, dispensing with all lawyers except himself, and deciding all cases and moving from county to county providing summary justice biased in favour of the poor. Edmund Ludlow confessed that to Cromwell 'Ireland was a blank paper' and that his 'supersedeas to the old courts there' would be an example from a 'younger sister' to an older, so that 'England might have been the learner and gainer by her' (*Memoirs of Edmund Ludlow*, 1.246–7).

Cromwell's campaign in Ireland in 1649–50 is the stuff of legend—legend rooted in part-truths. In forty weeks (from 15 August 1649 to 26 May 1650) he occupied twenty-five fortified towns and castles (and visited five more already in English hands) on a progress that began in Louth and moved through counties Dublin, Wicklow, Wexford, Waterford, Cork, Kilkenny, and Tipperary, and the east tip of co. Limerick. In other words he spent thirty-four of his forty weeks clearing Munster of royalist garrisons. He never moved north of Drogheda, nor south of Kinsale, nor west of Mallow. For the most part he followed up the ferocity at Drogheda and Wexford by startlingly generous surrender articles (as at Mallow, Fethard, and Kilkenny). Blood was shed on only five occasions even though several towns defied him for days or weeks (he was even forced by the atrocious weather and disease to abandon a siege of Waterford).

Two episodes from this phase of his career have given rise to the black legend: his sack of Drogheda and of Wexford. At Drogheda on 11–12 September Cromwell stormed a town that had refused a summons and his troops killed perhaps 3000 royalist troops in hot and cold blood, all the Catholic clergy and religious he could identify (mainly in cold blood), and an unknown number of civilians (probably all in hot blood). He followed the laws of war as they had operated in Ireland for the previous century and not as he had operated them in England. The royalist commander, Sir Arthur Aston, was clubbed to death, and 300 of his men, who had surrendered to mercy (that is, put their lives at the discretion of their vanquishers), were executed. Cromwell justified the massacre on three grounds. The first was by reference to the laws of war. The second was that it was as 'a righteous judgment of God upon these barbarous wretches who have imbrued their hands in so much innocent blood' (*Letters and Speeches*, 1904, letter 105, 17 September 1649). This was an inappropriate reference to the massacres of 1641–2: Drogheda had never been a confederate town and many of those killed—including most of the officers—were English, while the rest were men of Munster who had fought with Ormond against the rebels. And third, he justified the massacre on the grounds that it would terrorize others into immediate surrender and thus save lives in the long run.

In Wexford on 11 October his troops stormed a town still negotiating surrender articles (although with deliberate tardiness); again more than 2000 people were slain, including a larger number of civilians. The fact that as the assault began the defenders sank a hulk in the harbour, drowning 150 protestant prisoners-of-war, and that the Cromwellians found the bodies of more prisoners starved to death in a locked chapel, heightened their fury. Cromwell neither ordered nor sought to halt the indiscriminate killing that followed. Those soldiers who were not killed were sent to be slaves in Barbados. Drogheda was Cromwell's Hiroshima, and Wexford was his Nagasaki. These massacres did not bring an end to the war, only to atrocity. Resistance elsewhere led to more selective enforcement of the laws of war. At Gowran, for example, Ormond's own regiment surrendered on 21 March 1650. Cromwell ordered the officers to be shot but the common soldiers spared; and although he lost 2000 men at Clonmel in May, he offered and honoured generous terms to both town and garrison.

On 26 May 1650 Cromwell embarked at Youghal for England. His personal responsibility for the subsequent Irish settlement, and the 'Cromwellian confiscations', is very uncertain. Much hangs on the sincerity of his 'Declaration of the lord lieutenant of Ireland for the undeceiving of deluded and seduced people' (January 1650), in which he repudiated the claim made by twenty Catholic bishops gathered at Clonmacnoise that he had come to Ireland to 'extirpate the Catholic Religion'. Cromwell was withering in his denunciation of the episcopate in particular and of Catholic superstition and clerical tyranny in general (*Letters and Speeches*, 1904, 2.15). But while he stated that 'I shall not, where I have the power… suffer the exercise of the Mass', he also promised that:

> as for the people, what thoughts they have in the matter of religion in their own breasts I cannot reach; but I shall think it my duty, if they walk honestly and peaceably, not to cause them in the least to suffer for the same. (ibid., 2.16–17)

Summary executions would be visited only on those taken in arms; no other killing would take place except after trial by due process for cause known to the law; and he promised that only those in arms would be banished or transported. There was to be no general confiscation of property, other than that of men who were still in arms. Those who had long since laid down their arms could expect merciful treatment, those who laid down their arms immediately could expect some mercy, while such private soldiers as laid down their arms 'and shall live peaceably and honestly at their several homes, they shall be permitted so to do' (ibid., 2.22). There is nothing in Cromwell's declaration to suggest that he favoured different principles of retribution from those that had applied to the royalist party in England. It is far from clear how far he subsequently changed his view and supported the Act of Settlement of 1652 that envisaged up to 100,000 executions, and encouraged and even facilitated emigration on an unprecedented scale.

Quelling the Scots: Dunbar and Worcester

Cromwell was recalled from Ireland specifically to command the New Model Army—as commander-in-chief of all the land forces of the Commonwealth following Fairfax's resignation—in a war with the Scots. He had supported the policy of early 1649 to permit the Scots to resume the existence independent of England that they had enjoyed before 1603. Cromwell had no objection to their retaining monarchy for themselves. But he could not accept their determination to recognize Charles II as king of all Britain and Ireland and to fight to place him on all his thrones, and their determination to see confessional presbyterianism throughout the archipelago. When it became clear in the spring of 1650 that the marquess of Argyll was willing to commit Scottish arms to that enterprise and that Fairfax had no stomach to command against them, Cromwell was recalled. He was in London for only three weeks before setting off for the north on 28 June to launch a pre-emptive strike.

The harshness of the terrain and the climate, compounded by plague, had made the Irish campaign tougher than anything Cromwell had known. In Scotland he met fiercer resistance, was hindered by his own intermittent poor health, and, at least initially, made serious strategic errors. Entering Scotland late in July, he sought to bring to battle the swelling number of covenanters under Alexander Leslie, earl of Leven. But having stripped the Lothians of young men and all provisions, Leven was content to refuse him battle. Cromwell could neither afford to storm the strongholds, being unable to risk heavy casualties, nor to lock his army away in garrisons. Essentially he had not thought through what to do if Leven would not come into the field. He took out some of his frustration in a verbal attack on the Scottish presbyterian clergy at least as vicious as his attack on the Catholic clergy in Ireland. Accusing them of arrogance and 'spiritual drunkenness', he urged them to read 'the twenty-eighth of Isaiah, from the fifth to the fifteenth verse'. It was a passage which describes dissolute priests vomiting over the altar of the Lord. Theirs was, he said, not a covenant with God, but with 'carnal and wicked men'. Consider, he said, whether yours be a 'covenant with death and hell' (*Letters and Speeches*, 1904, letter 136, 3 August 1650). This was a phrase he had also hurled at the Irish bishops.

After a month, Cromwell's forces were depleted by desertion and disease to 11,000 and Leven's had grown to 22,000. Cromwell was stranded on the coast at Dunbar dependent on inadequate supplies from the sea. Leven occupied a strong defensive position cutting off his lines of retreat. It looked all too likely to be Cromwell's Lostwithiel. Leven (and the younger David Leslie, who was increasingly taking over from his ailing namesake) assumed he would try to break out with his cavalry and leave his infantry to make what terms they could. He was not prepared for what happened. For having got his strategy completely wrong, Cromwell displayed a tactical brilliance beyond anything shown by other commanders in these wars. Very early on 3 September, well before first light, he launched the greater part of his force against the right wing of the Scots, and having broken the stiff resistance of that wing, he wheeled to his right against the centre and eventually against the left of the Scots and destroyed them. It was the greatest of his victories. He claimed that 3000 Scots were killed and 10,000 were captured. Before the battle it was said that Cromwell was so tense that he bit his lips until blood covered his chin. He began the battle by emitting a great shout: 'let God arise and his enemies shall be scattered' (Psalm 51). After the battle, he laughed uncontrollably. Normally God had given the victory to the side that had providentially brought the greater number to the field. Never had God made himself so visible, so immanent. Cromwell's ecstatic letter to Speaker William Lenthall beseeched parliament to see how great was God's blessing upon them: 'God puts it more into your hands to give glory to him ... own His people more and more, for they are the chariots and horsemen of Israel. Disown yourselves, but own your authority'. They were, he added, to relieve the oppressed, reform the abuses of the professions (the lawyers and clergy), and 'if there be any one that makes many poor to make a few rich, that suits not a Commonwealth' (could this be a dig at the MPs themselves?) (*Letters and Speeches*, 1904, letter 140, 4 September 1650).

There followed twelve difficult months. Leslie's troops were holed up in very strong fortresses that Cromwell lacked the strength in depth to storm, and he himself was intermittently incapacitated by illness. Meanwhile the Scots were bitterly divided over how far to tie themselves to an unregenerate Charles II. When Cromwell was fit he oscillated restlessly between the Lothians and Strathclyde. He did occupy Leith and Edinburgh but he failed to lure Leslie back into a major engagement. With the embers of resistance in Ireland now extinguished, more men could be put into the Scottish theatre, and by July 1651 Cromwell felt able to send a force to occupy Fife and cut off David Leslie's connections to the highlands. He then moved the great bulk of his army north of Leslie's army with the deliberate intention of tempting him into a desperate invasion of England. On 4 August he wrote to Lenthall that although a Scottish dash on London 'will trouble some men's thoughts and may occasion some inconveniences' (*Letters and Speeches*, 1904, letter 180), it was preferable to another winter in Scotland with the Scots playing peekaboo with his army. Leslie swallowed the bait. He crossed into England on 9 August and headed south. Cromwell pursued, incorporating fresh English troops as he went, as Leslie shed his own. By the time they both reached Worcester, Cromwell had the same numerical advantage over Leslie as Leslie had had over him at Dunbar. On the anniversary of that battle, Cromwell won the inevitable and even more crushing victory, the 'crowning mercy' as he put it. Once again, his paean of praise for God's providential assistance led on to a demand that 'the fatness of these continued mercies may not occasion pride and wantonness as formerly, [but that] justice righteousness, mercy and truth may flow from you as a thankful return to our gracious God' (ibid., letter 183, 4 September 1651). Leaving others to mop up in Scotland, Cromwell returned to London on 12 September to be formally received in a triumph that echoed those of Roman generals, even Roman emperors.

The pursuit of stability, 1651–1653

6

At odds with the Rump

From the moment of Cromwell's return in triumph from Worcester he and his close colleagues in the army sought to galvanize the Rump. He had four objectives. First, he sought to persuade members of the Rump to set a time to dissolve itself and to hold new elections. Second, he sought to achieve a greater acquiescence from the large number of former royalists by a broad and generous amnesty. Third (and this was a change of heart), he supported the settlement that united the three former kingdoms into a single polity. And fourth (in the words of his declaration of 22 April 1653 justifying his dissolution of the Rump), he sought 'to encourage and countenance God's people, reform the law, and administer law impartially ... the fruits of a just and righteous reformation' ('A declaration of the lord general and his council', 1–2, *Writings and Speeches*, 3.5–8).

Immediately upon Cromwell's return the Rump abandoned its desultory plans to hold elections to recruit itself up to strength and began work on a bill for fresh elections. But the magnitude of Cromwell's problem can be seen in the fact that the house agreed on 14 November 1651 (though only by a majority of two and notwithstanding a passionate speech by Oliver) to fix a date for its own dissolution, but then to his dismay four days later settled on ending their sitting 'by' 3 November 1654, three years thence. After that the bill got caught up in a hundred procedural delays and prevarications.

Cromwell also gave his support to the proposal for an act of indemnity and oblivion that would safeguard all former royalists from any new proceedings for past actions. But again, while the principle was very quickly conceded, the devil entered into the detail and it finally emerged a much more pusillanimous act than Cromwell had hoped for and intended. And, over Cromwell's protests, the number of royalists named as 'malignants' and whose estates were to be sold to offset the debts of the state grew steadily, from 73 to 780.

Cromwell was also influential in the plans to incorporate Scotland into an enlarged English state. When he first set out on campaign there the plan had been only to occupy strong points in the lowlands and to create a cordon sanitaire for the future security of England. But as Cromwell encountered the factionalism and fanaticism of the hardline covenanters he became a convert to a union of the former kingdoms, although he hoped that the Scots would agree to a consensual union, and supported the proposal that delegates from the major shires and burghs, having first agreed to the principle of union, be sent south to take part in the agreeing of the detail. This turned out to be little more than a *fait accompli*. They were simply shown a draft bill and asked to comment on it before a final decision was made by the English council. The Rump wished to avoid a rhetoric of conquest and imposed union, but they made sure they got what they wanted.

It is far from clear what Cromwell's role was in the much harsher settlement imposed on Ireland. Under the Act of Settlement (September 1652) more than 100,000 Irish Catholics were made liable to the death sentence; all Catholics were made subject to penalties 'according to their respective demerits'; and no Catholic was to be allowed to reside, let alone to own property, in the provinces of Leinster, Munster, or Ulster, but would be herded into Connaught and co. Clare. Even then they would be liable to summary execution if discovered within 1 mile of the coast or of the River Shannon. This settlement was so much at odds with that envisaged by Cromwell in 1650 and with the policy he later pursued as lord protector that he probably disapproved strongly of it. S. R. Gardiner, the only scholar to study the passage of the legislation in detail, concluded that 'as far as the act of 1652 is concerned, there is no evidence whatsoever to connect it with Cromwell' (Gardiner, 'Transplantation', 707). It is more likely that the act was designed by Henry Ireton, law deputy from the time of Cromwell's departure for Scotland until his own death in 1651.

Dearest of all to Cromwell in these years, however, were those 'fruits of a just and righteous reformation' for which his letters from the fields of Dunbar, Inverkeithing, and Worcester had pleaded. Religious toleration was in place, and no one he approved of as 'honest' and 'godly' was suffering for his or her faith. But there was also concern to sustain a broad national church with no requirements as to forms of worship or pietistic practice, but with a loose definition of core beliefs (such as the fifteen 'fundamentals' of faith that a committee under Cromwell's chaplain John Owen proposed in the wake of the publication—in a translation in which John Milton had a hand—of the anti-Trinitarian Racovian catechism). He could also approve the Rump's intention to distinguish those beliefs that men and women could be allowed the freedom to evangelize from those that they should be required to keep to themselves; and he sought recognition of the principle that God's truth could be promulgated by persuasion but not by persecution. But parliament's failure to follow up Cromwell's plea to extend and adapt the evangelizing commissions for the propagation of the gospel from 'the dark corners of the land' to the whole of England, the failure to explore an alternative to tithes for the maintenance of the ministry, and the defeat of his proposal for a non-presbyterian rite of ordination all sapped Cromwell's patience. In essence, the Rump had done something towards embedding negative liberty, but little towards inculcating positive Christian liberty, the freedom of God's children to resist vice and embrace godliness through a programme of moral evangelism and of sanctions against the sins of the flesh. He felt much the same about the slow progress made with answering the call of his letter from the battlefield of Dunbar for an examination of inequities in legal process. He presided over the panel that appointed the extra-parliamentary Hale commission, but as its recommendations for reform of judicial process and of the substantive law of property began to come back to the Rump in the summer of 1652, they too ran into endless procedural delay.

Cromwell wanted an early end to the Rump, the hand of forgiveness if not of friendship to old enemies, fresh elections on a broad franchise, measures to promote godliness and equity. And beyond that? Did he want to see the restitution of some form of monarchy? Here above all the evidence is fragmentary, treacherous—and retrospective. And yet it cannot just be discounted. It takes two forms: one consists of the conversations Cromwell is said to have had with individuals and groups floating the idea of restoring the house of Stuart in the person of Henry, duke of Gloucester, still of impressionable years and in the hands of the regime. The other is the idea of Cromwell himself becoming king or at least occupying the kingly office.

The evidence for the former is to be found both in the known views of men to whom Cromwell was drawing closer at this time—especially Oliver St John—and in the testimony (probably near-contemporary) of Bulstrode Whitelocke in his *Memorials* that on 10 December 1651 Cromwell convened a meeting at which some present argued that the idea of a parliamentary grant of the title to Henry was feasible and desirable. Whitelocke records much said on both sides, but concludes that Cromwell summed up by saying that:

> this will be a business of more than ordinary difficulty! But really I think, if it may be done with safety, and preservation of our rights, both as Englishmen and Christians, that a settlement with somewhat of monarchical power in it would be very effectual. (Whitelocke, *Memorials*, 491–2)

As one historian puts it: 'before Worcester, the royalist threat had made it unthinkable that the Rump should voluntarily restore monarchy. Now the government could undertake such an initiative on any terms to which it could persuade the army to agree' (Worden, *Rump Parliament*, 276). If Cromwell's words were carefully recorded, then they were carefully chosen: 'somewhat of monarchical power' implies not necessarily a new king, but someone who would act as protector of a written constitution in the intervals between elected parliaments, someone who would prevent powerful legislatures from overreaching themselves, someone who was elected to ensure that the actions of executive bodies worked effectively. He had wanted no more in 1647 or 1648; he created that role for himself from 1653 to 1658. And it is worth linking this to the fact that at the time he made these remarks he hoped for an early dissolution and fresh elections. Perhaps he looked to a new, broader, elected parliament to negotiate this difficult but desirable outcome.

The belief that Cromwell was considering becoming king himself rests on the testimony of the disillusioned Edmund Ludlow, and on a further recollection by Bulstrode Whitelocke of a private conversation with Cromwell in Hyde Park in November 1652. Cromwell, Whitelocke recorded, expressed great weariness with the pride, sloth, and self-seeking of the Rump and then blurted out the question: 'what if a man should take upon him to be king?' Whitelocke's response was that there were far more difficulties in the way of such a move than in restoring the house of Stuart (*Diary of Bulstrode Whitelocke*, 281–2). But that the thought was in other sympathetic minds can be seen from the journal of a German diplomat, who wrote down at the time a conversation with John Dury, a key figure in the civil administration. Discussion turned to the adulation that Cromwell had received during his triumphal entry into London after the battle of Worcester. Herman Mylius had observed that perhaps Cromwell would be made England's doge: so great is he, replied Dury, that 'he is unus instar omnium, et in effectu rex' ('he is a man set above all others, and in effect, our king'; L. Miller, ed., *John Milton & the Oldenburg Safeguard*, *c*.1985, 49). It is unlikely that this was the only such conversation.

The Rump dissolved

By August 1652 Cromwell felt it was time to move on constitutionally, and that the fruits of the revolution were not being garnered in. His own patience was wearing thin, but that of the army was wearing thinner and Cromwell could feel the weight of their expectation. After a nine-hour meeting of the army council on 2 August 1652 the officers published their demands in the aggressively titled 'Declaration of the armie to the lord general Cromwell for the dissolving of this present parliament'. It called for an early dissolution and fresh elections, for a purge of unworthy men from the parochial ministry, the replacement of tithes, the implementation of the recommendations of the Hale commission, a non-parliamentary commission to look into corruption in public office, and a fundamental reform of taxation and of provision for the poor, and especially for ex-soldiers and war widows. Cromwell must have agreed with every word, but his reaction was to nudge the Rump into responding responsibly. Over the next few months he convened something like twelve informal meetings of leading officers and MPs. He tried his best, but he failed. Finally his self-restraint snapped and he undertook that which, he had told quartermaster John Vernon late in 1652, 'the consideration of the issue whereof made his hair to stand on end' (*Memoirs of Edmund Ludlow*, 1.346).

If Cromwell's letters from the fields of Dunbar and Worcester reveal his yearnings for constitutional settlement and godly reformation, then the Rump had utterly failed him. They had not disowned themselves but they had disowned their call to bring liberty and equity to the people; and the fatness of God's continued mercies had occasioned more pride and wantonness than righteousness, mercy, and truth. Cromwell's fundamental disappointment with them was further fuelled by new prevarications over a range of other issues. For example, he failed to persuade the house to address the £31,000 a month deficit on the army wage bill; and he was deeply irritated by their constant privileging of the adventurers and of friends of Rumpers over the army in the detailed arrangements for the redistribution of Irish land. He was losing patience, and was failing to contain the army's impatience. On 11 March 1653 he had to speak powerfully to defeat a vote in the council of officers to expel the Rump immediately. He did so by saying it would be easier to leave a dissolution until after a peace treaty was made with the Dutch. So it was added wormwood to him that he failed on 15 March 1653 to persuade the Rump to open negotiations. He ceased attending both the house and the council of state.

Despite all the warnings it had received, the Rump had no sense of urgency. Day after day was spent tinkering with the Irish Land Bill, and giving the bill for a new representative desultory attention. By 19 April Cromwell had had enough;

and he was well aware that many in the army were more exasperated than he was. Exactly as in 1649 he wanted due form to be followed if at all possible: the Rump's abdication was better than its deposition. He demanded that the Rump establish a caretaker government of forty drawn from itself and from the army, entrust all power to it as a constituent assembly, and then abdicate. He put this as something midway between a demand and an order to a cross-section of the members who sulkily agreed to suspend work on the new representative until his own plan had been debated. But the next morning, to his incredulity, Cromwell heard that they had gone back on their word and were debating a bill of their own. Four years of prevarication appeared to be being replaced by a day of defiant decisiveness. Arranging for troops to follow and wait outside the chamber, he went to the house and took his seat.

There were twice as many members present as usual, a clear sign that those who opposed his demand had called in all their friends. He was in a white anger and his words scourged his opponents one by one. With the help of about forty musketeers with lighted match, he cleared the chamber and carried off the mace and the papers that lay on the table. What precisely had been in the bill the Rump was rushing through is now irretrievable. In a declaration published two days later Cromwell claimed that they had done something even worse than continue with the bill for a new representative, and had reverted to the plan to recruit to themselves. This was probably a lie intended to increase the popularity of his act (although it just might have been a ghastly misunderstanding on his part). He dropped the claim once it had served his immediate purpose. If he was lying, it is the clearest occasion on which he can be shown to have done so.

Why should Cromwell dissolve the Rump when it was finally doing what he had so long demanded of it: making urgent arrangements for a new representative? It is likely that he thought the political tests to be applied to the electorate or to those eligible to sit were inadequate. It is likely that the bill provided for 'perpetual parliaments'—one damn parliament after another, each exercising full control over the legislative and executive activities of government, an arrangement that the Rump itself had taught Cromwell to be disastrous. It may have intended to make Rumpers alone responsible for vetting returns and deciding who was qualified and who was not qualified to sit in the next parliament. And it may be that the Rump's intention to delay its own dissolution until 3 November 1653 was intolerable to Cromwell in the light of the previous day's discussion. At any rate, he used strong language and brute force to dissolve the Rump. Cromwell had longed to see the back of it, but to the end he had hoped for an orderly transfer of power. When he acted as he did on 20 April he had no plan ready to implement. If he had wanted personal power then and there he could have taken it. His determination, in the days and weeks that followed, to avoid a leading role for himself is testimony to his lack of ambition.

The nominated assembly, July to December 1653

Instead, power passed immediately to the council of officers, and it was they who decided how to proceed from where they were. They set up a council of state of seven senior officers, headed by Cromwell, and six civilians to run civil government and foreign policy on a day-to-day basis. Meanwhile the council of officers themselves took responsibility for constitutional reform. They debated the merits of the scheme put forward by Major-General John Lambert for a council of state of forty with limited legislative powers and the plea of Major-General Thomas Harrison for a sanhedrin of saints. Harrison was a believer in the imminent second coming of Christ and the thousand-year rule of the saints predicted by the biblical books of Daniel and Revelation—the latter making the reconstitution of the Jewish ruling council of seventy men (the sanhedrin) a precondition of Christ's arrival. Few members of the council of officers subscribed either to this Fifth Monarchist package or to the fall-back position of Fifth Monarchist preachers like John Rogers that Cromwell was in a very real sense the new Moses chosen to lead the people of Israel from slavery in Egypt, through the Red Sea (regicide), across the desert to the Promised Land. But the council did like the idea of a constituent assembly made up of a cross-section of men drawn from 'the various forms of godliness in this nation', and Cromwell would seem to have been influential in giving precise shape to this assembly. He was, it is clear, behind the proposal that no serving army officer and no lawyer was to sit in the assembly. Gathered churches around the land, no doubt encouraged by what they heard, spontaneously sent in lists of names, but the council of officers seems to have acted principally on its own knowledge in the final nomination of 140 men to serve in the assembly. They were men of social substance—80 per cent were born into gentry families—and all had been active in the parliamentarian cause and were known for their commitment to religious liberty.

Neither in the writ of summons, nor in the place of its first meeting (the council chamber in Whitehall, not the parliament house in Westminster), nor in Cromwell's opening address is there any implication that the officers saw it as a parliament. It was an assembly, and its task was over a maximum period of eighteen months to prepare the people for the responsibilities of self-government.

From the years between 1653 and 1658 there survive what purport to be full versions of twenty-five speeches by Cromwell to the nominated assembly, to the protectorate parliaments, and to a committee of parliament seeking to persuade him to accept the title of king. Seven of these speeches (those of 4 July 1653, 4 and 12 September 1654, 22 January 1655, 17 September 1656, and 25 January and 4 February 1658) were major set-piece reviews of the political world as he saw it, and most took between two and three hours to deliver. They were printed or recorded verbatim, having the cadences of spoken rather than written speech. None of them was as upbeat, optimistic, and passionate as that of 4 July 1653. Cromwell clearly had the highest hopes for the nominated assembly. Far more than the others this speech is a sermon, containing significant meditations on passages from the Psalms, Hosea, Isaiah, and Romans. It began with a rehearsal of 'that series of providences wherein the Lord hitherto hath dispensed wonderful things to these nations, from the beginning of our troubles to this very day' (*Speeches*, 9). This section culminated in an analysis of why the dissolution of the Rump was just and necessary and how the army had lit upon the idea of the assembly. 'Truly God hath called you to this work by, I think, as wonderful providences as ever passed upon the sons of men in so short a time' (ibid., 20). He called upon them to:

> love all the sheep, love the lambs, love all and tender all, and cherish all, and countenance all in all things that are good. And if the poorest Christian, the most mistaken Christian, should desire to live peaceably and quietly under you, soberly and humbly desire to lead a life in godliness and honesty, let him be protected. (ibid., 22)

Then he charged them to come up with a reform programme that would turn the people from the things of the flesh to the things of the spirit, make themselves capable of taking responsibility for their own freedom. Towards the end the apocalyptic language intensifies and he called this 'a day of the power of Jesus Christ' (ibid., 23). But it was a this-worldly fulfilment of the promise of God to be with his people as he had been with Israel in their days of obedience; it was not evidence that Cromwell thought that the end of the world was nigh.

Cromwell then left the members to their own devices. They moved to the Commons chamber, announced they were a parliament, and began to act like one (hostile, royalist pamphlets soon lampooned it as Barebone's Parliament, after the name of one of its 'fanatic' members, the Baptist Praisegod Barbon). They invited Cromwell and three other officers to join them, but he firmly declined (although he did attend the council of state it set up to administer the Commonwealth day by day). As they wrangled and disputed, he just watched with dismay. Some radical bills were approved, but there was no progress on the essential matter that they had been constituted to address: a long-term constitutional arrangement that combined freely elected parliaments with advancing godliness and Christian liberty. By early December a clear majority of the members knew that they would not fulfil their commission. In collusion with Major-General Lambert—but not with Cromwell, whose protestation that he had no foreknowledge of it carries conviction—they voted themselves out of existence on 12 December and marched to Cromwell to tell him so. His experiment had failed.

Lord Protector, 1653–1658

7

The new regime

This time there was no great delay. Lambert had been preparing for this moment and stepped forward with a fully formed paper constitution, the 'Instrument of government', very clearly based on *The Heads of Proposals* of 1647. Senior members of the council of officers, including Cromwell, had already considered a draft of the 'Instrument', and Cromwell himself had insisted that the elected head of government should not be called king. But they were taken by surprise by the events of 12 December and over the next three days continued to refine the document in a series of long, tense, and inconclusive meetings. When Cromwell was formally sworn in as head of state on 15 December some passages of the 'Instrument' were not agreed, and had to be mumbled so as to be inaudible to the ambassadors and others present. It took several more days for the new constitution to be finally agreed and published.

For the remaining four years and nine months of his life Oliver Cromwell was to exercise as lord protector 'the chief magistracy and the administration of the government over [the Commonwealth of England, Scotland and Ireland and of the dominions thereunto belonging] and the people thereof' (Gardiner, *Constitutional Documents*, 406). As lord protector for life he had some freedom to act on his own, as in proroguing and dissolving parliaments once they had met for the prescribed minimum five-month period. He used this power in January 1655 and February 1658, on neither occasion consulting his councillors. But in most matters of governance he was constrained to act with and through the majority will of a council of state consisting of between thirteen and twenty-one members, over whose membership he had limited control. He and the council were given the authority to make law for the period before the next ensuing parliament, after which he would be required to make law in and through parliament, with a limited power of veto over bills approved by them. It was the council that selected and removed judges and all other civil magistrates.

Cromwell became lord protector on 16 December 1653. Between then and the meeting of the first protectorate parliament on 4 September 1654 he and the council of state ruled by decree, issuing 180 ordinances (only eighty-two of them published at the time), sixty of them in the fortnight up to 2 September. When parliament met, the council had plucked out about a dozen very obvious royalists as not being men 'of known integrity, fearing God, and of good conversation' (Gardiner, *Constitutional Documents*, 411). After some initial gestures of co-operation—such as approving without discussion all the appointments Cromwell had made that required their confirmation—parliament began a systematic review of the constitution. Cromwell, on the advice of the council, called them to a meeting and harangued them on how a 'cloud of witnesses' (a phrase from the epistle to the Hebrews) had underwritten the 'fundamentals' (*Speeches*, 42, 51; 12 September 1654). His cloud of witnesses included the army, the City of London, and all those who had written congratulatory petitions—even the MPs themselves, by seeking election on the writs of the protectorate. And the fundamentals were the separation of powers between protector and parliament, their joint control of the armed forces, that parliaments should meet for limited periods and were not 'perpetual', and religious liberty.

Cromwell then ordered all members to subscribe to a 'Recognition' of the protectorate. This caused about a quarter of the members to withdraw (ibid., 41–56). Parliament then worked on a solid body of 'Commonwealth' legislation (bills which regulated social, economic, and cultural life, dealing with such matters as parish boundaries and the local provision of welfare) and on a revised constitution, which would have given more power to parliament to clip the wings of the council, and which removed from Cromwell the right to veto bills 'agreed upon by the Parliament for the restraining of atheism, blasphemy, popery, prelacy, licentiousness, and profaneness; or such as shall preach, print, or publicly maintain anything contrary to the fundamental principles of doctrines . . . agreed upon by the Lord Protector and the Parliament' (Gardiner, *Constitutional Documents*, 443). All this was bundled up together to be offered as a package to Cromwell at the end of five calendar months. Cromwell, claiming that the reference to five months as the minimum duration of a parliament in the 'Instrument' meant five lunar and not calendar months, dissolved the house without warning on 22 January 1655 to prevent a showdown in which he would have had to reject their constitutional bill.

In the eighteen months before the summoning of the next parliament Cromwell was preoccupied with two matters above all. One—in the wake of the series of abortive royalist risings in late February and early March—was national security, and the introduction of the major-generals; the other was foreign policy. This was the period during which Cromwell was most active in the council. He took a close personal interest both in the efforts of the major-generals to encourage 'a reformation of manners' and in persuading a sceptical council to back the amphibious expedition against the Spanish West Indies.

The second parliament met on 17 September 1656, well before the triennial stipulation of article 11 of the 'Instrument', in order to provide taxation for the war against Spain. On this occasion the council ruled that more than 100 of those elected were ineligible, but the remainder chose not to make a fuss and for three months there was little friction within the house or between the house and the council. There was an unspoken agreement that Cromwell would leave them alone and that they would leave the constitution alone. He even kept out of furious debates during two weeks in December about how to deal with the Quaker James Nayler, whom many believed to have blasphemously claimed to be Christ (by riding into Bristol in imitation of Jesus's entry into Jerusalem on Palm Sunday). But behind the scenes a group of councillors and members of parliament were planning to bounce Cromwell into taking the crown, and they brought in a draft bill to this effect on 23 February 1657. For the next four months the house perfected a revised constitution built around a King Oliver. After much hesitation he rejected the crown but accepted the rest of the revised constitution, and after a period of equal hesitation parliament agreed to this compromise. Under the 'Humble petition and advice', a new upper house of Cromwell's own nominees would restore a bicameral parliament, Cromwell was given the responsibility of nominating his own successor, and the council was made more firmly answerable to parliament.

From July 1657 to January 1658 Cromwell, acting alone, struggled to give effect to the provisions of the 'Humble petition', and acting with the council he focused on the complex affairs of the Baltic and on the Spanish war. When parliament reconvened in January 1658, with the secluded members restored to the Commons and about fifty of Cromwell's friends translated to the upper house, it was clear there would be no co-operation, and after a short-tempered harangue had failed to recall them from determined constitutional obstruction (they challenged the title and powers of the 'other house'), he unceremoniously dissolved this, his last parliament. His final months were months of drift, except for a last great victory for British arms at the battle of the Dunes near Dunkirk on 4 June 1658. Cromwell's health deteriorated exponentially throughout the year and he died peacefully enough on 3 September.

The limits of authority

Too many studies of the period have assumed that almost everything that the three arms of government attempted and achieved while Cromwell was lord protector was the result of his initiative or had his consent. In fact he was often embattled and overborne by his councillors, by his parliaments, and perhaps by his army colleagues. This problem is compounded by a significant shift in the nature of the evidence about what Cromwell himself thought. The flow of private letters dries up once he had moved into the palaces of Whitehall and Hampton Court. It is replaced by the survival of full versions of about twenty-five public speeches. These certainly represent very personal, largely unwritten and unrehearsed expressions of passionate opinion, but their rhetorical structures and awareness of a wide audience are very different.

Cromwell's precise part in the shaping and articulation of government action is difficult to establish. There is no record of discussion at the council board; only its minutes of matters discussed and decisions reached are extant. He attended less than half of the more than 800 meetings up until his death—surprisingly, only a third of those in the period preceding the meetings of the first protectorate parliament (4 September 1654), and less than a third in the last nine months of his life. He was most attentive in the middle period of the protectorate, between the two parliaments (January 1655 to September 1656). At times it is hard not to conclude that he was deliberately absenting himself at a time of decisions with which he wished not to be associated (such as the selection of those to be excluded from the parliament as unqualified under the 'Instrument'). As head of state he did not attend parliamentary sessions. He formally opened and closed each session, and otherwise occasionally summoned the members to meet him on neutral ground such as the painted chamber within the palace of Westminster.

Cromwell was often dragged along reluctantly by what his councillors and principal officers of state advised him to do. The first fifteen councillors were named in the 'Instrument' and three more were soon chosen by Cromwell and the council in collaboration. The striking thing about the council is that it was not dominated by the army that established it. Only three senior officers (John Lambert, Cromwell's son-in-law Charles Fleetwood, and his brother-in-law John Disbrowe), together with Philip Skippon, elderly, retired, and largely apolitical, were among the eighteen. Three more were colonels who conjoined garrison commands with seniority in regional government. A clear majority were civilians, only one of whom—Henry Lawrence, his old landlord at St Ives in the 1630s—had a long and close relationship with Cromwell, although others had been allies in the Rump or had recently shown good sense during their time in the nominated assembly. They were a cross-section of the godly, essentially a band of strong Calvinists, although their ecclesiological preferences represented a spectrum from primitive episcopacy to Baptist. They were all men, in Cromwell's characteristic phrase, 'with the root of the matter' in them. Perhaps the most influential figure to emerge, however, is John Thurloe, who acted as sole secretary of state and head of the security services, a man whose instincts inclined towards normalizing government by the restoration of the kingship with Cromwell in it and towards gradually reducing the power and influence of the generals at court and of the army itself in the country.

Cromwell was constantly spending time discussing public affairs with a remarkable cross-section of preachers whose views he respected: a spectrum that ran from the former archbishop of Armagh, James Ussher, to the Quaker George Fox, all of whom found him a good listener and sincere discussant. But little is said, because little is known, about what happened at the weekly dinners to which Cromwell invited all army officers currently in London—up to 120 at any time. There was very little turnover in the officer corps (as against the rank and file) in the course of the 1650s. Almost a third of those who served as colonels in 1649 were cashiered for disaffection at some point in the 1650s, but they were replaced by men who were already majors or captains. So were these unminuted dinners an opportunity for reminiscence about battles won? Were they an opportunity for political lobbying and the pricking of Cromwell's conscience? Or were they an opportunity for him to get his colleagues to understand the complexity of the problems facing him and the integrity of his own and the council's response? Probably a bit of each. Certainly there are a few glimpses of how frustrated he could get when the army did interfere with politics. In an astonishing outburst to a deputation of 100 officers in London on 28 February 1657 he blamed them collectively for a series of miscalculations (he said they had made him their 'drudge upon all occasions'). And most notably he blamed them for the clumsy attempt to have the authority of the major-generals, the regional governors responsible for local security and 'a reformation of manners', placed on a statutory footing: 'who bid you go to the House with a bill and there receive a foil?' (*Speeches*, 111–12, 28 February 1657).

The protectorate consisted of two distinct phases divided by the great debate on the kingship (February to May 1657) and the replacement of the 'Instrument' by the 'Humble petition' (June 1657), under which Cromwell became king in all but name. In the first phase Cromwell represented himself more like the governor of Massachusetts than the king of England. He wore sober dark suits with collars unspotted with blood. His installation in December 1653 was very much a swearing-in, not a surrogate coronation, and in his short acceptance speech he put first among his tasks to make the gospel 'flourish in all its splendor and purity' (*Writings and Speeches*, 3.138). He took up permanent residence in the palace of Whitehall (Mondays to Thursdays) and Hampton Court (Fridays to Sundays). He endured being called 'his highness' (and allowed his daughters to take the title princess) and by 1656 he was dubbing knights, but the drift towards a monarchical style was slow and gradual. Evocations of royalty accelerated in 1657: his second investiture as lord protector (and there was no need for one beyond the taking of a new oath) self-consciously appropriated some aspects of a coronation and eschewed others. He sat in the coronation chair used since 1308, moving it to Westminster Hall from the abbey; he wore a robe of purple velvet lined with ermine; and he received a sword of justice and a sceptre (but not an orb or a crown). Henceforth his council was called a privy council, he created peers as well as an increasing number of knights, and his ritual behaviour on state occasions represented a dilution of royal practice.

Cromwell's public performance became more king-like. But whenever he described his own role he downplayed it. He described himself as a good constable, set to keep the peace of the parish. He likened himself to a watchman set on a watchtower to espy threats to security and peace. He reiterated that he had not called himself to the place that he occupied, saying that he saw it as a duty laid upon him by God and not as something he sought and enjoyed (*Speeches*, 40, 4 September 1654; 133, 13 April 1657; 174, 25 January 1658). With every speech there was less expectation that England was moving closer to the attainment of those things made possible by the overthrow of Stuart and episcopal tyranny, and more frustration at the lack of progress towards those goals. By the final speeches he was old, tired, and disillusioned.

In his speeches as lord protector Cromwell rarely drew on pre-civil-war history and never compared himself or his situation to that of English kings—or for that matter to continental kings or Roman emperors. There are a number of implied parallels between himself and Moses—especially extended metaphors about the people of England being like the people of Israel after the Exodus, 'repining in the desert'—and more obliquely between himself and David. Official publications, engravings, and the multiple copying of paintings by Peter Lely and Robert Walker emphasize his martial qualities and pedigree. Those currying favour and seeking to justify his actions again fail to draw on English history but are more evenly divided between biblical images of Cromwell (as Gideon, as Moses, or as David—only with his death did the image of Josiah, iconoclast, temple-restorer, and doomed warrior come into prominence) and images of Cromwell drawn from imperial Rome (Julius Caesar and Augustus predominantly, but also, in a double-edged way, Brutus). His critics focused on less deserving Romans such as Sejanus but by far the most favoured hostile typology was with the Machiavel.

Disillusionment and death

8

To what end?

Cromwell's attempts to realize his vision of a godly reformed nation abandoning the things of the flesh for the things of the spirit were constantly frustrated by those he was constrained to work with and through. He was frustrated with the council, which used its power under the 'Instrument' to remove far more of those returned to parliament than he wished, both in 1654 and in 1656. He was very reluctant to follow their insistence in the summer of 1656 that a parliament be called earlier than necessary. He was much more disillusioned by the failure of both parliaments to keep their eye on the task of providing the legislative framework for a reformation of manners, and by their interference with the rights of those who wished to exercise freedom of conscience outside the church. He was frustrated by the failure of the royalists to draw a line under the past and to accept that there would be no new penalties for old offences, and he was much more frustrated with the sects for refusing to live peaceably and quietly with one another and with the great number of sober, godly folk living out their lives in and around their parish communities.

All Cromwell could do was to mitigate the failure of all parties. When John Biddle was imprisoned on the Scilly Isles by the council for persisting in publishing anti-Trinitarian views, Cromwell made clear that he could not condone the public advocacy of such blasphemy, and would not overrule the council's decision; but in his horror of persecution he arranged for 10*s.* a week of his own money to be sent to Biddle to alleviate the conditions of his imprisonment. More dramatic was his intervention in the case of John Southworth, who was hanged, drawn, and quartered in June 1654, the only priest executed in Britain during the protectorate. Southworth had been condemned to death in 1627 under the Elizabethan laws making it treason to be a Catholic priest in England. His sentence had been commuted to perpetual banishment on pain of death if he returned. Arrested and identified by a pursuivant in June 1654 during a routine security sweep, he spurned the judge's advice that he refuse to confirm or deny that he was the same John Southworth (which would have allowed him to be released for lack of proof that he was) and he went to his death. Again Cromwell felt unable to overrule the court, but he did arrange for Southworth's quartered body to be reassembled and given to his seminary at Douai for Catholic obsequies. Indeed Cromwell's attitude to English Catholics was much milder than is usually recognized. He wrote to Cardinal Mazarin on 26 December 1656 and told him it was not politically possible to decree liberty for Catholics but that he personally had helped many to escape persecution and that he wanted to see an end to 'the raging fire of persecution, which did tyrannise over their consciences' and that he would, when he could, 'remove impediments' (*Writings and Speeches*, 3.368–9).

Catholics, like protestant sectaries, benefited from the repeal of all the statutes that required attendance at divine worship in their parish churches, and there was little disturbance of the private exercise of Catholic rites, even in central London. Cromwell operated a double tier of religious freedom. There was an active encouragement of those who came under the umbrella of evangelical protestantism and who affirmed the scriptures and the creeds; and a grudging acknowledgement of a right of unfettered private assembly granted to those who denied the authority of scripture or credal statements about the Trinity. Such groups were not in general compelled to witness against conscience, but nor were they allowed to proselytize their beliefs. This is one of the contexts in which to place Cromwell's strong personal advocacy of readmitting the Jews. He encouraged the Amsterdam rabbi Manasseh ben Israel, in his embassy to London, to plead for the formal readmission of the Jews, and when it became clear that a majority of the council would not support it Cromwell ruled that since their exclusion had been based solely on a royal edict, he could readmit them without consulting council or parliament.

Nothing caused Cromwell more pain or gradual disillusionment than his uphill struggle against the narrow-mindedness of a majority of MPs (and of his councillors) over the extension of religious liberty, especially given the continuing shrill demands for special privilege from so many of the sects. A comparison between his vision of 1653 and his nightmare of 1658 is especially poignant. He exhorted the nominated assembly to:

> be faithful with the Saints; to be touched with them ... In my pilgrimage and some exercises I have had abroad, I did read that Scripture often in Isaiah 41:19 ... what would [God] do. To what end? That he might plant in the wilderness the cedar and the [acacia] tree, and the myrtle and palm tree together. To what end? That they might know and consider and understand together that the hand of the Lord hath done this. (*Speeches*, 22, 4 July 1653)

It was a vision of 'the various forms of godliness in this nation' respecting one another, learning from one another, growing together in trust and love.

Eighteen months later, reproving the first protectorate parliament as he dissolved it, Cromwell said he had hoped that they would have 'upheld and given countenance to a Godly ministry, and yet would have given a just liberty to Godly men of different judgments'. Yet:

> is there not yet upon the spirit of men a strange itch? Nothing will satisfy them, unless they can put their finger upon their brethren's consciences, to pinch them there ... Is it ingenuous to ask liberty, and not to give it? What greater hypocrisy than for those who were oppressed by the bishops to become the greatest oppressors themselves so soon as their yoke was removed? (*Speeches*, 66–7, 22 January 1655)

And by January 1658 the irritation at the pinching of conscience had become something much more disturbing:

> What is that which possesses every sect? What is it? That every sect may be uppermost . . . we have an appetite to variety, to be not only making wounds, but as if we should see one making wounds in a man's side and would desire nothing more than to be groping and grovelling with his fingers in those wounds. This is what all men will be at . . . They will be making wounds, and rending and tearing and making them wider than they are. (ibid., 180–81, 25 January 1658)

Cromwell continued to aspire to see the law reformed, and in particular to see a greater equity and social justice introduced into legal proceedings. As he put it to his second parliament on 17 September 1656:

> The great grievance lies in the execution and administration . . . The truth of it is there are wicked abominable laws that will be in your power to alter. To hang a man for sixpence, thirteen pence, I know not what; to hang for a trifle and pardon a murder, is in the ministration of the Law, through the ill framing of it. I have known in my experience abominable murders quitted; and to come and see men lose their lives for petty matters. (*Speeches*, 99)

How far Cromwell personally influenced the parliament, or the council, or the judges, to address this beyond such exhortations is not clear. Perhaps significantly, this outburst immediately follows within the speech of 17 September 1656 his passionate defence of what the major-generals had achieved in respect to the 'reformation of manners'—by the stricter enforcement of the legislation against fornication, drunkenness, gambling, sabbath-breaking. He linked this campaign by a statement of his fundamental social conservatism, his desire to maintain the social order but to make every person more aware of the duties and responsibilities of their station:

> We would keep up the nobility and gentry; and the way to keep them up is, not to suffer them to be patronizers nor countenancers of debauchery or disorders; and you will be hereby but as labourers in the work ... The liberty and profaneness of this nation depends upon reformation, to make it a shame to see men to be bold in sin and profaneness. And God will bless you. (*Speeches*, 98)

In foreign policy, too, disillusionment gradually set in. Cromwell had a grand design in foreign affairs that he outlined to his second parliament: to use his influence and naval power to bring peace to protestant princes warring against one another (above all, peace among the Baltic protestant princes), and to renew the onslaught on Spanish power—'your great enemy is the Spaniard. He is. He is a natural enemy, he is naturally so' (*Speeches*, 81, 17 September 1656). He wanted peace with the Dutch, an alliance with France, and a war with Spain. Most of the details were left to the council. His own personal obsession, the expedition to seize Hispaniola (Dominica), was a disastrous failure, the occupation of Jamaica being taken as no substitute. Cromwell saw in that failure a rebuff from God, and it troubled him that God was displeased with him. But the hammering out of foreign policy cost him dearly. It led to serious divisions in the council, difficult and protracted negotiations, and unwelcome compromises. Thus the alliance with France, bearable because French protestants enjoyed a liberty of religion denied to subjects of the Spanish king, was utterly compromised when the duke of Savoy, a creature of the French government, undertook a massacre of his protestant subjects in the Valltelline in Piedmont. The worldly compromise over this matter that allowed Cromwell to remain in alliance with France troubled his conscience. As he lay dying, according to an anonymous letter to William Clarke, secretary to the army, he cried out 'what will they do with the poor protestants of the Piedmont, in Poland and other places' (*The Clarke Papers*, V, ed. Henderson, 272).

Cromwell took similar responsibility for the shaping of policy in Scotland and Ireland while leaving those on the ground and in his secretariat to work out the details. His concern at the very harsh settlement that the Rump had introduced into Ireland, reinforced by the tough militarism of Major-General Charles Fleetwood as lord deputy, led Cromwell to send his younger son, the assured and pragmatic Henry Cromwell, to bring an end to the plan to herd all the Catholics into the west of Ireland and to soften the policies against the Catholic religion and the participation of Catholics in trade and agriculture. More dramatically, it was very much at his own insistence that two men who had supported the king in Ireland in the period leading up to 1647—Major-General George Monck and Roger Boyle, Lord Broghill, younger brother of the earl of Cork—were won over to the Commonwealth regime in Ireland and then brought over to head the military and civil establishments in Scotland. Cromwell interfered counter-productively in the feuding among Scottish presbyterians, and gave too much authority over religion in Scotland to one faction of 'protesters' who lacked the strength in depth and social clout to be able to bring any stability.

100 Soldiering on

The protectorate was successful in achieving the widespread acquiescence of the English people, and towards its end there were only 6000 men in arms in England to maintain order. But Cromwell still needed 40,000 men to police Scotland and Ireland. The high taxation needed to fund them (and the expeditionary force serving with the French in Flanders, and by the time of his death garrisoning Dunkirk on a semi-permanent basis) nourished a low-level unpopularity of the regime. However much Cromwell might present himself in smart, sober, civilian clothes, he was still thought of as General Cromwell. The garrisons around the country were a law unto themselves: they were kept under strict and severe military discipline, but when their officers used them to menace civil magistrates into releasing Quakers from prison, or to assist in the distraint of taxes, or to press local freemen to vote a certain way in a local election, there was little civilian redress.

The abject failure of the royalist risings in the spring of 1655 showed how acquiescent the English had become, but it also showed how little active support Cromwell could count upon among the county élites. If few rose in arms to challenge the regime, few rose in arms to support it. Everyone outside the army waited upon events. Cromwell was persuaded by Major-General Lambert to embark on a bold experiment. If people disliked the regime because there were too many soldiers and too much tax, then let both be halved and replaced by efficient, well-trained and equipped 'select militias', made up mainly of demobilized veterans and paid for by a 10 per cent 'decimation' tax on the income of all convicted royalists. And let the scheme be under the management of eleven senior officers (the major-generals) each responsible for a bloc of counties, and assisted by bodies of activist shire commissioners. To Lambert's brief Cromwell added his own: they were to wage war on vice and promote the reformation of manners. It was in that aspect of their work that he took a close personal interest.

When the scheme came under remorseless attack in December 1656 and January 1657 it was principally because the major-generals, and the decimation tax they collected, were unconstitutional and against law and custom. To levy discriminatory taxation on ex-royalists was a clear breach of the Indemnity Act that Cromwell had campaigned for so vigorously in 1652. To levy taxation without parliamentary consent was against both the ancient and the modern constitution. There was a deep principle at stake here. If he and the council could arbitrarily tax ex-royalists, could he not arbitrarily tax everyone? In his speech of 17 September 1656 Cromwell tried to brazen it out:

> There was a little thing invented, which was the erecting of your major generals... we invented this, so justifiable [as] to necessity, so honest in every respect. Truly, if ever I think anything were honest, this was, as anything that ever I knew; and I could as soon venture my life with it as anything I ever undertook. (*Speeches*, 92)

The ends justified the means. There was in Cromwell no respect for the past, no sense of the integrity of the law, no legitimation to be found in antiquity or custom, just as there was no legitimacy to be found in majoritarian consent. God looked to the future not the past. His providences did not seal moulds but broke them. And God spoke through the remnant and not through the reprobate majority. Despite a longing for all to be freed from slavery to the flesh for freedom in the spirit, until that time came, legitimation would be found not in a hallowed past or a consensual present but a yearned-for future.

In this speech Cromwell defended not only the creation of major-generals and the levying of arbitrary taxes, but also the imprisonment of men without trial in gaols in the Scilly Isles and the Isle of Wight—beyond the reach of writs of habeas corpus. He defended the making of law outside parliament: 'if nothing should ever be done but what is according to law, the throat of the nation may be cut while we send for some to make a law' (*Speeches*, 100, 17 September 1656). A merchant called George Cony refused to pay customs duty on the silk he was importing on the strong ground that the protector's right to customs lapsed with the dissolution of the first parliament. To ensure that Cony lost the case, the council, with Cromwell's consent, imprisoned both Cony and his lawyers until they agreed to withdraw their suit. It was for attitudes such as these that the lawyers and pragmatic gentry of his second parliament sought to make him king. For (although given their wars with Charles I this was not without irony), a king was shackled by the past, required to act in accordance with ancient law and custom, and bound to seek the consent of the people through parliament in the making of law, the establishment of penalties, and the granting of taxation. Parliament's vote in December 1656 to have James Nayler publicly mutilated for his blasphemy only added to the cry for a return to known ways. Cromwell was shaken by their action, but powerless to prevent it. The timing of the offer of the crown, just after the Nayler affair and the debates on the major-generals, is indicative. Cromwell was in large part offered the crown not to further enhance his authority but to circumscribe the power of the protectorate itself, as well as the power of its ill-defined executive, legislative, and judicial bodies.

King Oliver

Rumours that Cromwell was to be made king can be found throughout the protectorate. Cromwell had aired it with Bulstrode Whitelocke late in 1652, but he ruled it out when it was in the first draft of the 'Instrument'. Yet rumour continued to flourish. For example, the Swedish ambassador sent a long dispatch home on 1 June 1655 carefully laying out twelve arguments for and three against Cromwell's becoming king: his prediction was that Cromwell would assume the title shortly thereafter. So it was not a bolt out of the blue when Alderman Sir Christopher Packe, acting for a group within and far beyond the council, proposed on 23 February 1657 that Cromwell be king under a contract that modified the terms of the 'Instrument', strengthening his personal authority as against that of the council but prescribing his power in relation to the ancient constitution and unshackled parliaments. Indeed, he was to have one new power greater than that of the old monarchy: the freedom to nominate his own successor. Cromwell from early on indicated a willingness to accept everything except the title. Parliament tried to bluff him into it by maintaining it was all or nothing. In the battle of wills that followed the house cracked first. Cromwell was to become king in all but name.

 Cromwell spoke to the Commons, or to its negotiating committee, on nine occasions between 31 March and 25 May 1657. There is no reason to doubt his agony of mind and conscience. It is true that his colleagues in the army, those he had fought alongside in battle after battle, lobbied relentlessly against the title. It is not right, however, to conclude that he was intimidated out of becoming king. Intellectually, he was fully persuaded: 'I am hugely taken with this word "settlement"' (*Speeches*, 144, 21 April 1657); 'I cannot take upon me to refel [refute] those grounds, for they are strong and rational' (ibid., 129, 13 April 1657). Yet his conscience would not give him leave: 'it would savour more to be of the flesh, to proceed from lust, to arise from arguments of self-love . . . it may prove even a curse to these three nations' (ibid., 136, 13 April 1657). He waited upon a clear sign from God (a great victory over the Spaniard?) and it never came:

> God has seemed providentially not only to strike at the family but at the name . . . He hath blasted the title . . . I would not seek to set up that which Providence hath destroyed and laid in the dust, and I would not build Jericho again. (ibid., 137, 13 April 1657)

And so he turned it down. He just could not see how it could be God's will that he accept the title. But five times in his speech of 13 April 1657 (*Speeches*, 128–37) he repeats: God has blasted the title and the name. But what of the office that the name signified? Would God have the kingly office renamed, as he had had the jurisdiction of bishops in the primitive church retained but in offices which no longer bore the name of bishop? Could he, Cromwell, discharge the duties and responsibilities of king as the earthly surrogate of Jesus, the only true king? This tortured logic may have persuaded him to be king-like in power and display but without the blasted title. God would have his vicar ruling, an upper house consisting of a spiritual aristocracy nominated by this vicar-protector, and a restoration of that which could bring healing and settling to a still-broken people.

Cromwell's death and its aftermath

Then the dusk of life closed in, and with the dusk a sea-mist. The last few months were months of idling. Cromwell's health declined steeply, and he became much preoccupied by the terrible suffering and death from cancer of his beloved daughter Elizabeth. Despite rumour at the time that what the assassin's bullets had failed to achieve, insidious poisons did achieve, it is overwhelmingly likely that the malarial fevers that had troubled him at time of stress ever since the early 1630s came back to haunt him and triggered a chest infection and pneumonia from which he died. Alternating between fevered dreams and moments of lucidity, he died at Whitehall at three in the afternoon on 3 September 1658, on the anniversary of the 'eminent mercy' at Dunbar and the 'crowning mercy' of Worcester.

Under the 'Humble petition and advice', Cromwell had the duty to nominate his successor. There was no other mechanism for the transfer of power. Amazingly there was no written designation. John Thurloe reported that he had been told that there was one sealed up but that he could not find it. Can Cromwell have been so careless? He had seen too much of sudden death to be unmindful of his own mortality. Indeed he carried a loaded musket with him whenever he went out for fear of assassins and once, in 1654, he almost killed himself when his musket exploded as he was dragged behind some bolting horses. Conspiracy theories—that Thurloe broke the seal of the written nomination, did not like what he read in it (the likely names were John Lambert or Charles Fleetwood), and destroyed it—should not be lightly dismissed. However, recent discoveries in the shorthand letters of William Clarke strengthen the case for Cromwell's having made a lucid and clear nomination of his eldest surviving son, Richard, in the presence of witnesses, during his final hours.

After his death a wooden effigy of Cromwell with a wax mask lay in state at Somerset House vested with his robe of estate, a sceptre placed in one hand, an orb in the other, with a crown laid on a velvet cushion a little above his head. The ceremony was modelled on the lying-in-state of James I. Thus was Cromwell crowned in death, his scruples no longer carrying weight. The fact that it was not Cromwell himself was because he had been incompetently embalmed. When the body began to putrefy it was decided to proceed rapidly with burial; it was secretly interred, probably on 4 or 5 September in Westminster Abbey. It was thus the effigy, not the corpse, which made a sombre and ill-planned progress on 23 November through the streets of London—largely deserted, say the contemporary diarists, all predisposed to wish it so—so that it arrived at Westminster Abbey at nightfall; and no-one had organized candles. So there was no ceremony in the abbey. The coffin was placed on a sumptuous catafalque—again based on Inigo Jones's design for that of James VI and I—in Henry VII's chapel in the abbey.

There Cromwell remained—his body and his effigy, presumably—until after the Restoration. Then the vengeful Convention Parliament decreed that he, like others who signed the king's death warrant, should suffer the fate of traitors. It was decided that Cromwell, Ireton, John Bradshaw, and Thomas Pride should be exhumed and their bodies desecrated on the twelfth anniversary of the regicide, 30 January 1661. For reasons never adequately explained except by conspiracy theorists, Cromwell's body was removed from the abbey on 26 January and moved to the paddock behind an inn in Holborn. From there it was taken to Tyburn on 30 January. Unsurprisingly it has long been claimed that this was to allow another body to be substituted for his actual body (Bradshaw's body was brought directly from the abbey, his grave being opened only on 29 January). A body purporting to be Cromwell's was hanged in its cerecloth for several hours, then decapitated. The body was put into a lime-pit below the gallows and the head, impaled on a spike, was exposed at the south end of Westminster Hall for nearly two decades before being rescued during the exclusion crisis. Descendants of his daughter Mary have the best of several similar claims that the bodies were exchanged and that Cromwell's undivided body lies in their family vault in Newburgh Park, near Coxwold in the North Riding of Yorkshire. Another, and stronger, tradition has the skull rescued from Westminster Hall in or about 1688 and surviving with a fairly complete itinerary—as a fairground exhibit, or one brought out at dinner parties in great houses—until it was acquired by Cromwell's descendants and by them donated to Sidney Sussex, Cromwell's college in Cambridge, where it was interred in an unmarked grave in 1960.

Posthumous reputation

9

Early responses

Cromwell's reputation has ebbed and flowed. Since the death of the generation that knew him as their head of state more than 160 full-length biographies have appeared, and more than 1000 separate publications bear his name. In 1929 Wilbur Cortez Abbott, limbering up to produce his four-volume, 3400-page, 2-million-word edition and commentary, *The Writings and Speeches of Oliver Cromwell*, produced a bibliography of 3520 pamphlets, books, and essays in which Cromwell makes a prominent appearance. An updated list would probably be in excess of 6000 items. There was a crescendo of interest in the later nineteenth century, triggered by the appearance of Thomas Carlyle's edition of Cromwell's letters and speeches in December 1845.

It had not been ever thus. In the immediate aftermath of Cromwell's death several journalistic biographies appeared, together with Henry Daubeny's edgy attempt to find thirty lengthy parallels between Cromwell's life and that of Moses.

There was then a moment of republican scorn in the winter of 1659–60 which was overtaken by sensationalist synthetic royalist rage. This reached its apogee in James Heath's *Flagellum* (6 edns, 1662–81), but from the 1660s Cromwell's name rather dropped into the background. Fewer titles invoking it appeared between 1663 and 1700 than in the years 1660–63. The whigs did not seek to rehabilitate him and the tories used him as a bogeyman more than as someone whose career needed rehearsal. When there was a brief revival of interest in the 1690s it took the form of hostile parallels between Cromwell and William III: such parallels were promoted both by Jacobite authors and by those deist-republicans around John Toland who re-edited the work of Edmund Ludlow to highlight the parallels between the two military 'tyrants'.

As personal memory faded and death carried away those who could testify from experience, and with the tracts of the 1640s and 1650s locked away in private libraries and little known to a new generation of pamphleteers, Cromwell became less known than at any later period. When Britain became once more sucked into major wars in the 1690s with the mobilization of huge armies and a financial and administrative revolution to sustain them, memories of the previous military dictatorship were revived by the publication of the memoirs of many of the men at the heart of the period: to those of Bulstrode Whitelocke (1682) were added between 1696 and 1704 those of Richard Baxter, Edmund Ludlow, and Denzil Holles, and Clarendon's *History of the Rebellion*. This represents a wonderful cross-section of opinion. All (with the exception of Ludlow) were men who both admired and deplored Cromwell. Their memoirs set the tone for eighteenth-century discussions. Gentlemen of letters were unanimous in seeing him as dangerous and fanatical, although the degree of his self-interested dissimulation differs as between the unrelieved contempt of the tories and the regretful whigs. John Hampden and John Pym, fortunate in the time of their deaths, were the respectable witnesses against royal and episcopal tyranny. As David Hume put it, Cromwell was the 'most frantic enthusiast ... most dangerous of hypocrites ... who was enabled after multiplied deceits to cover, under a tempest of passion, all his crooked schemes and profound artifices' (Richardson, 64–5).

There was a blunter, unvarnished literature generated within and for the dissenting communities that recognized his strivings for a religious liberty grounded in religious and civil egalitarianism. There were, above all, three biographies, by Isaac Kimber (1724), John Banks (1739), and William Harris (1762), which were never noticed outside dissenting circles but may well have been influential within them. Thus while it is not easy to find Cromwell being evoked in any systematic way in any political campaign during the radical awakening of 1770–1830 (although the bogey of regicide was used by government agents against both the Wilkites in the 1770s and the Foxites in the 1790s), Elizabeth Gaskell could write that in the nonconformist villages of the West Riding in the 1820s the phrase 'in Oliver's days' denoted a time of prosperity, and in 1812 an anonymous threat was sent to the government noting that 'it was time a second Oliver made his appearance' (Richardson, 99).

Carlyle and his successors

The transformation of Cromwell into a dominant figure in British public memory can be closely linked to the publication of Thomas Carlyle's *Letters and Speeches of Oliver Cromwell* in December 1845. It was to remain continuously in print in inexpensive editions for exactly 100 years. At a conservative estimate more than 100,000 copies were sold, and many were handed down from generation to generation. Thomas Macaulay had begun the process of rehabilitation twenty years before, but Carlyle's edition took the world by storm. It is a passionate defence of Cromwell's sincerity, of his faith in God, in his living out his vocation and his mission. Carlyle's Cromwell had a contempt for democracy, an unreflective belief in spiritual aristocracy, a rough-tongued, cloudily articulated integrity. Deficiencies of scholarship and Carlyle's own obtrusive interpolations disfigure his text, but did not dull its impact. It emboldened the views of Congregational historians like John Forster who had earlier taken a more cautious line on Cromwell. Now—in the best available summation of Carlyle's Cromwell—he hailed the new Cromwell as:

> no hypocrite or actor of plays . . . no victim of ambition, no seeker after sovereignty or temporal power. That he was a man whose every thought was with the Eternal—a man of a great, robust, massive, mind and an honest, stout, English heart. (Lang, 133–4)

One unintended consequence of Carlyle's edition was certainly to make Cromwell the champion of a particular denomination—Congregationalism—and of its history. His preference for a broad national church with a public ministry within which the great majority would hear the word of God, sing his praises, and submit themselves to gentle correction for their sins passed the Victorians by. He became first and foremost the spokesman for Victorian middle England and of responsible self-reliant nonconformity. It is striking that when in 1899, for the very first time, commemorative events to mark a major Cromwellian anniversary were held, they were all organized through and controlled by the Congregational and Baptist churches. At the London ceremony David Lloyd George proclaimed that he believed in Cromwell because 'he was a great fighting dissenter' (*The Times*, 26 April 1899, 12). Rather more preposterously, another nonconformist MP, R. W. Perks, claimed on the same occasion that:

> the modern equivalent of the seventeenth-century Puritan, was the possessor of the Non-conformist conscience, who now raised his voice against the desecration of the Lord's Day, against the gambling saloon, the drink bar, the haunt of vice, and the overwhelming power of brute force. (*The Times*, 28 April 1899, 8)

In addition the tercentenary of 1899 also stabilized Cromwell's academic reputation. Both Samuel Rawson Gardiner and Sir Charles Firth wrote biographies. Supervised by Firth, Mrs S. C. Lomas re-edited Carlyle, checking and correcting his transcriptions and adding more than 200 pages of material that had come to light since 1845. It was unfortunate that this edition—welcome though it was and is—appeared more or less simultaneously with a truly scholarly edition of the speeches by C. L. Stainer (based on an Oxford DPhil dissertation). That edition remains the benchmark and finally gained acceptance when used as the basis of Ivan

Roots's popular edition in 1989 (though without Stainer's scholarly apparatus). This, together with the new editions—mainly by Firth—of many little-known papers in which Cromwell played a prominent part (the Putney debates, rediscovered by Firth in 1890, and the memoirs of Lucy Hutchinson and Edmund Ludlow), brought a new solidity to Cromwell studies. In the course of the twentieth century the American scholar W. C. Abbott undertook a fundamental new edition of all Cromwell's words on the page and in reported speech. Unfortunately, his scholarship was sloppy, his way of organizing the material requires the patience of saints from all its users, and Abbott became one of several leading scholars shallowly convinced that Cromwell was a forebear of the Fascist dictators. So a great opportunity was missed.

Since 1945 Cromwell biographies have become gradually more sympathetic in tone. Even Christopher Hill, who in *God's Englishman* (1970) portrayed a Cromwell who came increasingly to betray the revolution he had done so much to create, rooted himself firmly within Cromwell's own terms of reference and self-representation. For that was the key. The twenty most widely read biographies—from John Buchan's and Antonia Fraser's accounts aimed at a general readership, through Robert Paul's account, which echoes at a high level of sympathy and engagement the denominational tradition of the nineteenth-century Congregationalists, to those aiming principally at a student audience (the most recent of which are those of Barry Coward, Peter Gaunt, and J. C. Davis)—work within a very clear set of conventions. The authors have read all the letters (some 500 of which can be confidently said to have been Cromwell's own work), twenty major and many minor speeches, and the much less reliable summaries by others of what he is reported to have said. They weigh the evidence of his self-representation against the testimony of contemporary tracts and of personal memoirs. All the serious biographies have drawn on very similar bodies of evidence. And although the judgement of the vast majority of his peers is harsh in its assessment of his honesty, integrity, and credibility, historians have opted to take him much more at his own valuation, finding in his words an openness and striving that usually appeals and just sometimes appals.

Images and memories

Yet throughout the period during which Cromwell's reputation in England was gaining ground, his name was becoming reviled in Ireland. For the first 200 years after the conquest he had been subsumed in Catholic—at least in English-language Catholic—writing in a long list of English men of violence, and in ascendancy writing his religious fanaticism relegated him as hero to a status far below that of King Billy. But with the recovery of Irish-language folklore in the nineteenth century, and with the emergence of a new kind of Irish nationalism, Cromwell was demonized. This new harsh view was adumbrated in J. P. Prendergast's *The Cromwellian Settlement of Ireland* (1865), and reinforced by Father Denis Murphy's *Cromwell in Ireland* (1883), a book which became the basis of a century of Irish school textbooks, popular novels (of which Walter Macken's best-selling *Seek the Fair Land*, 1959, was the culmination), and popular songs (such as 'Once upon a Time', sung by Sinéad

O'Connor at a demonstration outside the British embassy in Dublin in August 1989).

Cromwell was memorialized not only in print but on canvas, in woodcut and engraving, and in marble and bronze. He is one of the most familiar of Englishmen, more familiar to more people certainly than all but a handful of English monarchs or British public figures. The first statue of him by Matthew Noble was erected in Manchester in 1875 followed by three more statues in his tercentenary year: the Hamo Thornycroft statue erected outside the palace of Westminster after testy parliamentary debate in 1899; in Warrington a statue presented by a local businessman, which shows Cromwell addressing his troops and Scottish prisoners after the battle of Preston, a statue which inappropriately has 'Holy Bible' engraved on the back not the front of the book he is holding; and perhaps the finest of them all, the statue by Frederick William Pomeroy in St Ives, raised opportunistically after the town council of Huntingdon had declined it. The statue by Thornycroft of Cromwell, Bible in one hand, sword in the other, which has stood on Cromwell Green since the tercentenary of his birth in 1899, is one of the most visible and noticeable statues in the country. The contemporary portraits by Robert Walker (two of them), Samuel Cooper (four miniatures), and Peter Lely have been endlessly reproduced not only in lives of Cromwell but in lives of the men and women of his time. They in turn inspired many of the 750 engravings listed by W. C. Abbott in his catalogue which includes work noticed by him in 1930. The vast majority show him as a soldier, as a martial man of God, evoking (sympathetically or unsympathetically) his puritanism, either through the characteristic plain style of his collars protruding from his armour or his holding of a Bible. There was at least one Victorian Staffordshire pottery figurine manufactured as a chimney ornament; but it does not seem to have caught on. More surprisingly he is memorialized in stained glass, in prominent windows in the Victorian Congregational church in St Andrews Street, Cambridge, and in the chapel of Mansfield College, Oxford.

Cromwell is memorialized musically. A folk-song bearing his name was edited by Benjamin Britten in 1938. A nursery rhyme which can be first traced back to the late seventeenth century begins 'Oliver Cromwell lay buried and dead, hee-haw, buried and dead', and tells how his wraith rose and 'gave a drop' to an old woman gathering apples that had fallen on his grave. The most extraordinary musical evocation is undoubtedly the rendering of a John Cleese prose poem by the Monty Python team (on the recording *Monty Python Sings*, 1989) that tells the life of Cromwell set to the music of a polonaise by Chopin.

Cromwell is memorialized institutionally. Isaac Foot, a prominent Liberal politician of the 1920s and 1930s, established in 1935 the Cromwell Association. It has always had a membership of hundreds rather than of thousands, but it has worked effectively to extend knowledge and understanding of Cromwell and of his age. It has erected memorial plaques on battlefields and other Cromwellian sites; it has promoted publications about Cromwell and has held competitions to encourage the study of Cromwell by adults and children; and it holds an annual service of thanksgiving by the Thornycroft statue. The association in its early days collected many artefacts associated with Cromwell and these, together with a larger group owned by his descendants, form the basis of the collection held by the Cromwell Museum, which is in the Huntingdon schoolroom he once attended. The house he owned in Ely is also a museum, and an information and education centre. The Cromwell Association and the Cromwell Museum jointly set up a website in 1999 which promotes his memory and jointly co-ordinated the activities of more than thirty museums, galleries, and sites during the Cromwell quatercentenary year. It is doubtful if any other non-royal Englishman is so diversely commemorated.

Cromwell is also memorialized by name. George V prevented Churchill, as first lord of the admiralty, from naming a battleship the *Cromwell* in the First World War, but royal influence was less persuasive elsewhere. The first colleges established by the Congregational Church for training ministers in Australia, Canada, and South Africa bear his name. More than 250 roads in Britain bear his name, in all the metropolitan boroughs except for Birmingham and in most county towns; a great majority of these roads and streets comprise Victorian or Edwardian terraces, the backbone of late nineteenth-century nonconformity (though Cromwell Road in South Kensington was given its name at the suggestion of Prince Albert). No lay person other than Wellington approaches him in this respect. On the other hand, on the 400th anniversary of his birth on 25 April 1999 only three inns and public houses bore his name, although there were more than 400 websites on the internet bearing it. These included one devoted to Cromwell as an exemplar of good family values, one devoted to exploring his institutionalized violence against the people of Ireland, several devoted to making available key passages from his letters and speeches, and one devoted to commemorating a black slave who had been given the name Oliver Cromwell and had been decorated for his courage in the American Civil War.

Cromwell's role in fiction is also extensive. The earliest play bearing his name was George Smith Green's *Oliver Cromwell: an Historical Play* (1752), followed by the anonymous *Cromwell, or, The Days of the Commonwealth* (1832). He is the hero of Victor Hugo's melodrama *Oliver Cromwell* (1828), although it seems that a 1923 London production was the play's first staging in England. Six other plays that either bear his name or in which he is the central figure were staged in the West End (most of them in the 1920s). He was the anti-hero of Henry William Herbert's *Oliver Cromwell: a Historical Novel* (1838), and he had more than a walk-on part in Alexandre Dumas's *Vingt ans après* (1845)—a sequel to *The Three Musketeers*, Captain Marryat's children's classic, *Children of the New Forest* (1846), James Kirke Paulding's *The Puritan and his Daughter* (1849), by an effectively anti-British American writer, and G. J. Whyte-Melville's *Holmby House* (1860). In all of them he is a grim, unsmiling, self-righteous puritan, a literary equivalent of 'When did you last see your father?' In contrast most Victorian realizations of civil-war scenes in which he appears, such as Daniel Maclise's *Interview between Charles I and Cromwell*, Ford Madox Brown's *Cromwell on his Farm*, or Edward Croft's *Cromwell after Marston Moor* show him as grim, determined, but virtuously purposeful. Although actors playing Cromwell have appeared in a number of feature films (such as Alan Howard's portrayal of him in *The Return of the Musketeers*), only one feature film has been made specifically about him—*Cromwell*, which improbably cast the Irish tearaway actor Richard Harris as the hero (although Alec Guinness's charismatically prim Charles I stole the show). But Cromwell has been the subject of much television drama, from John Hopkins's *Cruel Necessity* in 1962, in which Patrick Wymark bore an uncanny likeness to him, onwards. Between 1985 and 2006 at least nine programmes devoted to him were produced for British terrestrial television. He remains one of the most recognizable of Englishmen.

10 Conclusion: God's true servant

Recognizable for what? Cromwell was not a great thinker. In 1638 he told his young cousin that 'if here I may serve my God either by my doing or by my suffering, I shall be most glad' (*Letters and Speeches*, 1904, letter 2, 13 October 1638). It was his motto and his epitaph. He did not enjoy power. It was thrust upon him. He was not especially intelligent, and was quite unintellectual, lacking a deep understanding of law, of the classics, of theology. He had a deep sense of being propelled by God into leading his people towards a promised land. He had an imperfect sense of what the promised land would look like, and only a magpie instinct for picking up the latest bright and shiny idea of how to make the next move towards it. Those whose ideas he took up all too briefly felt the warm glow of his approval. He then moved on to the next idea, and abandoned the people as well as the ideas that had not worked. This is why he was so resented and so distrusted by those he affirmed and then abandoned—John Lilburne and Charles's intimates in 1647, the Independent politicians in 1648, Sir Henry Vane in 1653, Thomas Harrison in 1653, John Lambert in 1657. He could never make the adjustment from war where the objective was always clear and the victory unambiguous. The pragmatism and compromise of the political arena constantly dismayed him and ground him down.

All this cost him in personal terms. He yearned to 'keep a flock of sheep under a woodside', to emulate Gideon who led the armies of Israel and then returned to his farm. But God would not let him go. God would have him serve. And still there was before him the mirage of a perfected humanity. He had seen that corrupted institutions could not deliver a humanity more obedient to the will of God. He was called to overthrow tyranny and pride and replace it with humility and a common concern to share the fragments of truth that so many men of goodwill had been granted. But instead pride and self-interest kept on taking over. As he climbed another barren hill and peered over the next sun-baked valley, the mirage reappeared. What makes Oliver Cromwell endlessly appealing and endlessly alarming is that he was true to his own vision. He never doubted his call to service or to salvation. He knew enough of the Bible to know that all those whom God called, he chastened. The fierceness of his determination to free all those whose sense of God shared elements of his own experience drove him into uncomfortable action. He was not wedded and glued to forms of government. He was not bound by human law. If God called upon him to be the human instrument of his wrath, he would not flinch. His sense of himself as the unworthy and suffering servant of a stern Lord protected him from the tragic megalomanias of others who rose to absolute power on the backs of revolutions. Cromwell's achievements as a soldier are great but unfashionable; as a religious libertarian great but easily mis-stated; as a statesman inevitably stunted. No man who rises from a working farmer to head of state in twenty years is other than great. To achieve that and still to be able to say that 'if here I may serve my God either by my doing or by my suffering, I shall be most glad' is a man of towering integrity. He was to himself and to his God most true, if at great cost to himself and others.

Sources

The letters and speeches of Oliver Cromwell with elucidations by Thomas Carlyle (1845–) [cited by item no., which remains constant] · *The letters and speeches of Oliver Cromwell*, ed. T. Carlyle and S. C. Lomas, 3 vols. (1904) · *Speeches of Oliver Cromwell*, ed. I. Roots (1989) [based on the texts prepared for an Oxford DPhil by C. L. Stainer, pubd 1901] · *The writings and speeches of Oliver Cromwell*, ed. W. C. Abbott and C. D. Crane, 4 vols. (1937–47) · W. C. Abbott, *Bibliography of Oliver Cromwell* (1929) · J. Heath, *Flagellum, or, The life and death, birth and burial of O. Cromwell, the late usurper*, 4th edn (1669) · J. Bruce and D. Masson, eds., *The quarrel between the earl of Manchester and Oliver Cromwell*, Camden Society, new ser., 12 (1875) · *The Clarke papers*, ed. C. H. Firth, 4 vols., Camden Society, new ser., 49, 54, 61–2 (1891–1901) · *The Clarke Papers*, V, ed. F. Henderson, Camden Society, 5th ser., 27 (2005) · *The diary of Bulstrode Whitelocke, 1605–1675*, ed. R. Spalding, British Academy, Records of Social and Economic History, new ser., 13 (1990) · [B. Whitelocke], *Memorials of the English affairs* (1682) · *The memoirs of Edmund Ludlow*, ed. C. H. Firth, 2 vols. (1894) · S. R. Gardiner, *Constitutional documents of the puritan revolution, 1625–1660*, 3rd edn (1906) · P. Gaunt, *A Cromwellian gazetteer* (1987) · P. Gaunt, *Oliver Cromwell* (1996) · J. C. Davis, *Oliver Cromwell* (2001) · J. S. Morrill, ed., *Oliver Cromwell and the English revolution* (1990) · B. Coward, *Oliver Cromwell* (1991) · R. S. Paul, *The lord protector: religion and politics in the life of Oliver Cromwell* (1958) · R. Howell, *Cromwell* (1977) · C. Hill,

God's Englishman: Oliver Cromwell and the English revolution (1970) · C. H. Firth, *Oliver Cromwell and the rule of the puritans* (1900) · S. R. Gardiner, *Cromwell's place in history* (1898) · P. Warwick, *Memoires of the reign of King Charles I* (1701) · J. Buchan, *Oliver Cromwell* (1934) · A. Fraser, *Cromwell, our chief of men* (1973) · J. Gillingham, *Portrait of a soldier: Cromwell* (1976) · A. Woolrych, *Oliver Cromwell* (1964) · C. H. Firth, *Cromwell's army*, 3rd edn (1921) · J. P. Prendergast, *The Cromwellian settlement of Ireland* (1865) · D. Murphy, *Cromwell in Ireland: a history of Cromwell's Irish campaign* (1883) · T. Reilly, *Cromwell the honourable enemy: the untold story of the Cromwellian invasion of Ireland* (1999) · J. S. Wheeler, *Cromwell in Ireland* (2000) · T. Barnard, *Cromwellian Ireland*, rev. edn (2000) · J. D. Grainger, *Cromwell against the Scots: the last Anglo-Scottish war, 1650–1652* (1997) · C. H. Firth, ed., *Scotland and the Commonwealth: letters and papers relating to the military government of Scotland, from August 1651 to December 1653*, Scottish History Society, 18 (1895) · D. Stevenson, *Revolution and counter-revolution in Scotland, 1644–1651*, Royal Historical Society Studies in History, 4 (1977) · F. D. Dow, *Cromwellian Scotland, 1651–1660* (1979) · I. Roots, ed., *Cromwell: a profile* (1973) · J. Morrill, ed., *Reactions to the English civil war, 1642–1649* (1982) · S. R. Gardiner, *History of the great civil war, 1642–1649*, new edn, 4 vols. (1893) · A. Woolrych, *Britain in revolution, 1625–1660* (2002) · C. Holmes, *The eastern association in the English civil war* (1974) · A. Woolrych, *Soldiers and statesmen: the general council of the army and its debates, 1647–1648* (1987) · M. Mendle, ed., *The Putney debates of 1647: the army, the Levellers and the English state* (2001) · J. Peacey, ed., *The regicides and the execution of Charles I* (2001) · R. Ashton, *Counter-revolution: the second civil war and its origins, 1646–8* (1994) · I. Gentles, *The New Model Army in England, Ireland, and Scotland, 1645–1653* (1992) · S. R. Gardiner, *History of the Commonwealth and protectorate, 1649–1656*, new edn, 4 vols. (1903) · C. H. Firth, *The last years of the protectorate*, 2 vols. (1911) · G. E. Aylmer, ed., *The interregnum* (1973) · C. Jones, M. Newitt, and S. Roberts, eds., *Politics and people in revolutionary England* (1986) · D. Underdown, *Pride's Purge: politics in the puritan revolution* (1971) · B. Worden, *The Rump Parliament, 1648–1653* (1974) · D. Norbrook, *Writing the English republic* (1998) · S. Kelsey, *Inventing the republic* (1997) · A. Woolrych,

Commonwealth to protectorate (1982) · R. Sherwood, *The court of Oliver Cromwell* (1977) · R. Sherwood, *Oliver Cromwell: a king in all but name, 1653–1658* (1997) · C. Durston, *Cromwell's major generals: godly government during the English revolution* (2001) · S. C. A. Pincus, *Protestantism and patriotism: ideologies and the making of English foreign policy, 1650–1668* (1996) · T. Venning, *Cromwellian foreign policy* (1995) · L. Knoppers, *Constructing Cromwell: ceremony, portrait and print, 1645–1661* (2000) · T. Lang, *The Victorians and the Stuart inheritance* (1995) · R. C. Richardson, ed., *Images of Oliver Cromwell* (1993) · P. Karsten, *Patriot heroes in England and America* (1978) · D. Armitage, 'The Cromwellian protectorate and the languages of empire', *Historical Journal*, 35 (1992), 531–55 · G. E. Aylmer, 'Was Cromwell a member of the army in 1646 and 1647 or not?', *History*, 56 (1971), 183–8 · A. N. B. Cotton, 'Cromwell and the self-denying ordinance', *History*, 62 (1977), 211–31 · C. H. Firth, 'The court of Oliver Cromwell', *Cornhill Magazine*, new ser., 3 (1897), 349–64 · C. H. Firth, 'Cromwell and the crown', *English Historical Review*, 17 (1902), 429–42; 18 (1903), 52–80 · J. McElligott, 'Cromwell, Drogheda and the abuse of Irish history', *Bullan* (2002) · J. Morrill, 'Textualising and contextualising Cromwell', *Historical Journal*, 33 (1990), 629–39 · G. Nuttall, 'Was Cromwell an iconoclast?', *Transactions of the Congregationalist Historical Society*, 12 (1933–6), 51–66 · D. Piper, 'The contemporary portraits of Oliver Cromwell', *Walpole Society*, 34 (1958), 27–41 · A. Woolrych, 'The Cromwellian protectorate: a military dictatorship?', *History*, 75 (1990) · B. Worden, 'Toleration and the Cromwellian protectorate', *Persecution and toleration*, ed. W. J. Sheils, Studies in Church History, 21 (1984), 199–233 · A. B. Worden, 'Oliver Cromwell and the sin of Achan', *History, society and the churches*, ed. D. Beales and G. Best (1985), 125–45 · S. R. Gardiner, 'The transplantation to Connaught', *English Historical Review*, 14 (1899), 700–34 · P. Gaunt, 'To Tyburn and beyond: the mortal remains of Oliver Cromwell', *Cromwelliana* (1986) · P. Gaunt, ed., *Cromwell 400* (2000) · M. Noble, *Memoirs of the protectoral house of Cromwell*, 2 vols. (1787) · J. Waylen, *The house of Cromwell* (1897)

Index